To Jim and Gragella
"May God bless you
in all you do. Hope you
win a MILLION in Vegas.

Your's & Goodman
"The Miracle Man"

Jan/02

Proverbs 3:6
"In everything
you do put God
first and He will
crown and direct
your efforts with
success"

THE MIRACLE MAN

An Inspiring Story
of Motivation and Courage

THE MIRACLE MAN

An Inspiring Story of Motivation and Courage

Morris Goodman

MIRACLE MAN PRODUCTIONS, INC.

© 1991 By

MIRACLE MAN PRODUCTIONS, INC.

Library of Congress Cataloging in Publication Data

Goodman, Morris.
  The miracle man.

  Bibliography: pp. 221–222.
  1. Goodman, Morris.   2. Quadriplegics—
Virginia—Biography.   3. Motivation (Psychology)
            II. Title.
RC406.Q33G66 1985   362.4′3 [B]   84-22896

ISBN 0-13-585357-5

Printed in the United States of America

DEDICATION

This book is dedicated to all the great motivators who have laid the groundwork and explored much unfamiliar territory, which enabled me to overcome insurmountable odds. And to all the people in the helping profession—doctors, nurses, research people, therapists—who represent the sweat equity of generations. To them I owe so much, and it is my hope that, through this book, I can help repay some of my debt.

ACKNOWLEDGMENTS

An ancient Chinese proverb says that everyone you meet makes a mark on your paper of life. My deepest appreciation goes to the following people who have made marks on my paper of life.

Family: To my wife Sandy who stood by me through all my turmoil and trauma; to Pat Waldo, my sister, who went far beyond the call of duty under most trying times; to Sam and Jeanette Fink, my father and mother-in-law for never giving up on me; to my dear departed mother Dare, who proved that there is no love quite like a mother's love; and to all my other relatives that stood by me and came to visit.

Friends: To my dear friend Landon Browning, who did more than a brother would; to Doug Martin, for all his help with my business; to Mel Friedman and Joe Leibowitz, for all their help with getting my financial and legal affairs straightened out; to Fred Day, my business associate, who stood by me; to Bill Hermann, Karl Steen, Dr. Thomas Voshell, and all the members of the Norfolk Life Underwriters Association for all their cards and visits; to Page Scott and Ray Taylor for pulling me from the plane and saving my life; and to my dearest friend of all, Dr. Leonard Oden, who is more like a father to me than a friend.

Medical Profession: To Dr. Berkley Rish, whose skill as a neurosurgeon is second to none; to Dr. Richard Whitehill, who took over my case when I was transferred to Charlottesville; to Dr. Thomas Spicuzza and Dr. Richard Auld, for all their care during my rehabilitation at Woodrow Wilson; to all the nurses at Norfolk General Hospital, the University of Virginia Hospital, The Towers, and Woodrow Wilson for all their loving care; to Duane Anderson, my counselor at Woodrow; to everyone who worked so hard with me on my therapy, Yaffa Liebermann, Lorna Christenson, Julie Westerhaus, Dave Sum-

7

mer, Diane Petry, and Meg; to Ruth Bogart, my private duty nurse, who helped me more than I can ever repay; and a special thanks to Dr. Jack Kenley, the most caring and dedicated physician I have ever come in contact with.

Help with Book: To my dear friend Zig Ziglar, who gave me encouragement to get started with writing this book and helped me organize it in the beginning; to Frank E. Sullivan, CLU, for all his help and inspiration; Gerhard and Laura Gschwandtner for bringing everything together and working around the clock to get this project off the ground and the manuscript sold; and to Pat Garnett, a most gifted writer, for all her help in making this book more readable.

FOREWORD

This is the true story of one man's courageous fight against total paralysis, and his victory over unbelievable odds! In a story of being and becoming, this man conquered his personal "Mount Everest."

Epictetus, a Greek philosopher, wrote: "Men are not moved by things, but the views which they take of them." And on that tragic day when Morris Goodman's plane crashed and he embraced death, his life took an unexpected turn. Facing a life of total paralysis from the neck down, most people are devastated beyond description! They close their eyes in shock and disbelief, only to open them to find an overwhelming tide of anger, frustration, grief, guilt, depression and emptiness. These crippling waves of emotions are the aftermath of crushed lives, broken dreams and empty tomorrows. But Morris Goodman chose not to focus on these things, but instead propelled himself toward creating new dreams and new tomorrows!

Gail Sheehy, in her book, *Pathfinders*, describes how people who are "Pathfinders" overcome life's crises and find well-being. As Morris Goodman's rehabilitation counselor, I have been most fortunate to have shared in a small part of this process. This book allows others to share in it also.

This is the true story of one man's incredible journey through tragedy to rehabilitation and beyond.

Duane Anderson
Rehabilitation Counselor

TABLE OF CONTENTS

chapter **1**

TO LIVE

There are no hopeless situations;
There are only men who have grown hopeless
about them.

ANONYMOUS

Floating above the grassy field, I felt the exquisite serenity of a soul freed from earthly cares. His voice was familiar, yet different from anything I had ever heard; comforting, but also stern, like a loving parent's explanation of an unwelcome rule; forceful but not frightening. I felt it as much as heard it, although I had no sense of my own physical being—or His.

The voice came from above and behind me as I looked down upon the gruesome scene. I tried to turn around, tried to see who owned the voice, but could not. With an air of peaceful detachment, I viewed the rescue squad, their prognoses filling the air with death, and a state trooper, awaiting the exact time when life would end, his pen poised, his pad in hand, ready to absorb the ink of expiration. My limp and mangled body lay shrouded in blood. The trauma team was fighting for my life. And the voice would not let me rest.

"You must return to your body. There is much unfinished work for you to do," came the unwanted command.

I did not want to leave my peaceful state, but I had no time to think about it.

Instantly, I had the sensation of breathtaking speed, conscious of moving through a pitch black tunnel toward an intense light. Filmlike projections of my life pierced the darkness, flickering ever faster. The images were sharply divided, as if by a surgeon's knife. To my left were vivid scenes of happiness and success—a quail retrieved by my first bird dog, Mutt; my acceptance by Metropolitan Life as a full-time insurance salesman; my entrance into the Million Dollar Roundtable; passing my private pilot's license test; my first fishing trip on my new boat, *Miss Sash*. And to my right, countering these pleasant pictures, were equally striking specters of death and dying—my father's final hours; my Uncle James after his heart attack; poor old Mutt being put to sleep; the demolished car I escaped from 15 years earlier; the funerals of two other uncles whom I had dearly

14

loved. As I approached the tunnel's end, the images blurred with a sense of unrelenting speed.

Now conscious of the ambulance, I was alive again. Traveling from the airfield near Cape Charles, Virginia, to Nassawaddox Hospital, Ray Taylor, a paramedic, was saying, "Hang in there, buddy; you're going to be okay." Then came the pain—the excruciating pain. Every bump was a torment of agony engulfing me in the cruel reality of my broken body.

After a frantic examination at Nassawaddox Hospital, the medical team there decided that I needed the facilities of a larger hospital if I were to have any chance at all of surviving. It would be risky, though. The 40 mile trip to Norfolk General Hospital might be too much for me. Thank God they decided it was worth a try. I was put back into the ambulance and off we went.

We were traveling slowly, to minimize my suffering, when my blood pressure and pulse fell to life-threatening levels. Pain was secondary now. "You better speed up, he's not going to make it," I heard someone say. Racing along at close to 100 miles an hour, we met a police escort at the end of the Chesapeake Bay Bridge-Tunnel, and, at last, the torturous ride to the hospital was over.

The team of over a dozen highly skilled trauma professionals was awaiting my arrival. My family physician, Dr. Andy Fekete; a kidney surgeon and friend, Dr. Eugene Poutasse; and a gifted neurosurgeon, Dr. Berkley Rish, joined the emergency medical staff. The X-rays from Nassawaddox were reviewed, and it was discovered—for the first time in this nightmarish journey—that my neck was broken.

That fateful day began like a beautiful dream. It was March 10, 1981. Less than 24 hours earlier, I had bought my own plane, a Cessna 172. Driving across the Chesapeake Bay Bridge-Tunnel that afternoon, I recalled my first solo flight. (I'd had only a few hours of instruction under my belt, but I was performing practice landings flawlessly that day.) After a while my instructor, Harold Tarkington, taxied back to the runway, then pulled off onto the grass and hopped out.

"What in the world are you doing?" I asked.

"She's all yours," Harold replied.

"Wait a minute. I'm not ready for this!" I protested.

"You'll do just fine," said Harold. "Remember to use your

carburetor heat, square your patterns, and stay at 800 feet and everything will be okay." With that, he latched the door. "I'll be watching, and if everything looks okay, I'll wave to you, and you can try another landing."

The plane was facing downwind at the intersection of two runways. I was supposed to taxi to the active runway and take off into the wind. In my excitement, I forgot. There I was, racing down the runway at full power with the wind *behind* me, the trees rapidly approaching, and the plane would not lift off. Closing my eyes, I yanked on the stick as hard as I could. The plane finally left the ground, but I felt a jolt and heard all kinds of noises.

When I opened my eyes, tree branches were hanging from the wings. My heart was beating like a runaway freight train. Glancing at the altimeter, I saw that I'd climbed to 3,000 feet. Leveling off, I tried to calm down. In a heart-to-heart talk with God, I said I'd think twice before I ever got in an airplane again—if I ever got my feet back on the ground! Somehow I calmed down enough to land. After bouncing all over the runway, I finally got the plane stopped.

There was Harold, standing in the middle of the runway, waving his arms frantically.

"You want me to go around again?" I asked. Harold's reply is unprintable. I guess I'd done enough damage for one day.

Well, I kept my promise not to tempt fate—for a while. But then I began to rationalize, as we all do. If I could handle that crisis, I could handle anything. I started taking lessons again, got my license, then worked on my instrument rating and completed that phase of my training.

After that first solo flight, I experienced my share of engine stalls and shaky takeoffs. Yet the exuberance I felt while skimming ocean waves and soaring through brilliant blue skies transcended all fear.

A friend of mine, Doug Martin, had planned to fly with me that Tuesday. But an unexpected business meeting altered our plans. I headed toward my date with destiny—alone.

It was a clear, calm day—perfect weather for a journey over paradise. Page Scott, a farmer and friend who owns a small grass-landing strip, had my plane gassed and ready to go. Taking off my coat and tie, I was raring to be airborne. After a preflight check, I started the engine and taxied into position for takeoff. Soon the wheels yielded their grip on earth, and I was flying, free and majestic as a Canada goose. I leveled off at 800 feet, heading for the Chesapeake Bay. As I crossed Cherrystone Creek, I was struck, as always, by the beauty of the landscape unfolding below me—wild and unspoiled. The scene brought back memories of days spent hunting and fishing for its natural treasures. One day I will own a piece of this land, I thought to myself. I will build a home overlooking the water and spend my last years here in this heaven on earth.

I turned north, continuing up the bay toward Kellam Field. A smooth landing onto the limited grass strip, 18 gallons of fuel, and I was off again. Heading seaside, I reached the Barrier Islands—lovely strips of sand and coastal greenery—where I descended to 25 feet, almost skimming the water. This always gave me the feeling of a gull swooping along the cresting waves.

When I reached Fisherman's Island, I climbed to 800 feet and headed for home. The sun was setting, reflecting off the water—a million diamonds just for me. I was at peace with the world.

Five minutes later, Scott Field came into view, and I prepared for my landing. After circling the field to check for wind direction, I set up my approach. It was a tricky spot to land on; the runway was only 1,300 feet long and required letdown over telephone wires, so the approach had to be slow. I reduced my speed to 75 mph and added 20 degrees of flaps. Turning final, I added full flaps and held 2200 RPMs, reducing my speed to 65–70 mph. Everything was going smoothly.

Without warning, the engine lost power. The RPMs fell to 800. I saw the wires looming ahead at windshield level. A soaring shorebird just ten minutes ago, I was now a hunk of metal hurtling toward earth. So this is what it's like to die, I thought. Without a trace of panic, I added full power and reached to retract the flaps, determined to avoid the fate being forced upon me. The engine would not respond. Cursing like a Marine, I reeled through the power lines and watched the nose of the airplane and the ground meet. Everything went black.

Below, on the airfield, unnoticed by me, Page watched my approach. Realizing that I was too low to make the wires, he frantically shouted, "Get it up, Morris, get it UP!" Page ducked behind his house, alerted by an eerie hissing, just in time to escape a high voltage cable as it whipped through the air, still attached to a metal transponder. With a thunderous roar, the cable crushed the side of his daughter's car.

Ray Taylor was in Page's hangar working on his own plane when he heard the roar and realized the power had gone off. He ran outside to see what the problem was. The sight that greeted him was a nightmare.

What was left of the plane lay upside down. Upon impact it had flipped over, and the wings had struck the ground flat. Each wing contained a gas tank. Incredibly, they had not ruptured. Sparks were everywhere; wires entangled the aircraft like a black widow's web. Several lines had set the grass on fire.

Grabbing a fire extinguisher, Page rushed to put out the fire before it reached the plane. Then he cut off the master switch and ignition switch to prevent any electrical current from starting another blaze or creating an explosion.

"Help me ease him through the windshield!" Page yelled to Ray. Together they pulled me from the wreckage, laying me on the ground.

Page ran to call the rescue squad and a local doctor. Ray immediately began mouth-to-mouth resuscitation. I was dead upon impact, and he was trying to breathe new life into my limp body. It took a nerve-racking five to seven minutes before my body responded to his efforts. Just as Page hung up the phone, it rang.

"What time will Morris be home for dinner?" my wife, Sandy, wanted to know. Page, a usually calm, unflappable guy, was frantic.

"Morris has been in a plane crash, and the ambulance is on the way. Talk to Mary; I've got to get back to the airfield!" cried Page as he thrust the receiver at his wife. He raced back outside while Mary told Sandy that she would be there to pick her up in about 45 minutes to take her to the hospital.

Within minutes of the crash, the rescue squad and Dr. Thomas Hardman arrived from the small town of Cape Charles. I was swiftly lifted into the ambulance, and we set off for Nassawaddox, 15 miles away. Twenty-two minutes after the crash, I was wheeled into the emergency room.

I had been dead; had felt set apart; had seen myself, broken and bloodied, lying in the emergency room at Nassawaddox.

Now I was alive. As I was being transferred to Norfolk General Hospital, then wheeled into the emergency room, I could hear the concern and fear in my friends' voices. I sensed the urgency in the hospital staff's movements. The pain was becoming unbearable. But I kept telling myself that I would make it.

To slip away into the peaceful painless sleep that we call death would have been so easy—everyone expected it. The rough ride to Norfolk General should have severed my crushed spinal cord. Half the muscles and ligaments in my neck were destroyed. My neck was broken at the first and second vertebrae. My jaw was crushed, and it felt as if every bone in my face was fractured. But I had not broken a single tooth! My mouth must have been wide open upon impact; I had been cursing that plane all the way to the ground.

My larynx and voice box were crushed—I couldn't speak. The nerves in my diaphragm were so badly damaged that it wouldn't work, so a tracheotomy had been performed (a tube was inserted through an incision in my throat), and a respirator was connected to the trachea tube. I couldn't breathe on my own.

I was unable to swallow—that reflex was also severely damaged—so I was put on intravenous feeding. My bowels, bladder, and kidneys weren't functioning.

If I did live for more than a few days, the prognosis was grim: a living vegetable.

I knew that it would take time, determination, and courage to overcome the odds of survival. It would have been easy to buy a ticket for the first flight out—death. The price would have been cheap. But I'm not a buyer; I'm a seller. I kept selling myself on the fact that anybody could take that journey of escape. To hang in there, though, and make a battle of it would be a tremendous challenge. If the angel of death was coming for me, he'd better be prepared for the fight of his career.

Without hesitation, I made up my mind. I chose to fight for life. And, as anyone who knows me can attest, once I make up my mind to do something, there is no changing it. All my life, I have been accused of being hardheaded—it's probably true. But once I've decided on a plan of action, a goal, I will move heaven and earth to achieve it. The ability to zero in on one goal and concentrate 100 percent of my mental energy on it is the principal reason I am here today.

When the ambulance arrived at Norfolk General, a large crowd of friends and relatives had gathered at the emergency room doors. Through a chain of calls, most of those dear to me had heard of the accident and had come to do what they could. The person removed from that ambulance must have come as quite a shock to everyone. I was hardly recognizable—bloodied and swollen face, black eyes, bloated neck.

My mother's doctor was among those hoping for some word on my condition. The sight of me confirmed his worst fears; I would probably die, soon. It might mean my mother's death as well. Over the last few years, she had suffered a stroke and several nervous breakdowns. Surely this would kill her.

With great courage, my sister, Pat Waldo, left to pick up Mother, knowing she might be ushering her to a sudden death. She turned to her friend, Pat Webb, and my Aunt Herzberg, saying, "I guess we'll have a double funeral. We'll bury my brother, and the next day we'll bury my mother." When my sister returned with Mother, she asked Pat Webb to check on my condition. If I had died, she would need to prepare Mother first. The looks of grief and sympathy would be too much of a shock. It was going to be chancy even if I were still alive. Pat Webb returned to the car.

"He's alive, but his condition is extremely critical," came the somber report.

At some point, while in Norfolk General's emergency room, I must have passed out. The next thing I remember was awakening to a scene right out of a science fiction thriller. Wires were connected to my body, linking me to strange machines that flashed and whirred and hummed, filling the small dark room with an other-world aura. Was I still alive? Yes. With the help of these metallic creatures, my bodily functions were all being maintained—breathing, pumping, circulating, monitoring. My brain could not cope with the chaos of neural impulses and the inoperative organs so vital for life.

At first only my wife and sister were allowed to visit me in this twilight world of the intensive care unit. Sandy's face assured me that I was still on earth. The fright and sadness were real. I could hear and was fully aware of what was being said, but I could only blink my eyes to show them that I knew they were there. Dr. Rish had told them on March 14 that I was not aware of anything and couldn't respond to any of their questions.

"You know you're going to die, don't you?" my sister said. My eyes shot wide open in shock and disbelief.

"He does understand, he does!" Pat shouted to the doctor as she ran down the hall. "I just told him he was going to die and scared the devil out of him!"

"He's psychotic," replied Dr. Rish. "He can't understand a thing you say."

This was to be the first of many instances when I functioned far beyond the expectations of my doctors. They were basing their opinions on test results and past cases. I was basing my expectations on sheer will: a will to live and a will to recover fully.

The classic concept of positive thinking—a deep belief in the unlimited potential within each of us—vaulted me to the pinnacle of sales success before my accident. In 1980 I was eligible for the exclusive Top of the Table Club. I was one of the top 300 insurance agents in the free world. That year the club's requirement for eligibility was $8 million worth of permanent insurance sold. I had set a personal goal of $15 million for 1981 and was well on my way to meeting that mark—$4 million sold and paid for and another $4 million underwritten—at the time of my accident. But such success seemed highly unlikely during the summer of 1970. I was a college dropout, lacking direction and purpose.

The turning point came when I purchased a paperback book written by Napoleon Hill, *Think and Grow Rich*. The book sat in my room, untouched, for a week. But once I picked it up, it became an obsession. I was hooked after reading the first ten pages. I didn't sleep until I'd finished the entire book. Then I read it a second time, underscoring key words and phrases. The third time through, I took notes. The book's message was simple. Whatever the mind of man can conceive and believe, it can achieve.

Some of my relatives were in the insurance business, and I was aware of their success and fine standard of living, but up to then I'd avoided committing myself to any line of work. Could I measure up? I'd never thought of myself as a salesman.

After reading and rereading Hill's book, I was sure I could do whatever I *told* myself I could do.

Test scores showed that I had no aptitude for sales, yet the tests had no way of measuring ambition, persistence, initiative, drive, motivation, attitude, and hundreds of other intangibles. The more people told me I *couldn't* sell insurance, the more positive I was that I *could*. My Uncle Myer Herzberg took pity on me and arranged an interview with Fred Bashara of Metropolitan Life, after other companies had told me I was just not cut out for this. If Fred had judged me on my appearance alone, that would have been the end of that. I showed up with hair down over my ears, wearing navy blue pants, a pink sports coat, a striped shirt, and a striped tie. I must have said the right things, though, because he agreed to give me a try. I didn't disappoint him. I made the Million Dollar Roundtable— only about one in every 150 insurance agents qualifies annually—during my first year in the business.

In 1973 I became interested in tax and estate planning, so I began reading and studying everything I could find on the subject. Colleagues warned me that I would need a transition period of several years before I could make a full-time salary from it. Nevertheless, I stopped selling life insurance and got through a ten-week changeover, drawing little income. My company threatened to fire me. But my determination paid off. I doubled my production that year, and it steadily increased every year thereafter.

Now, however, life was the prize, not a new account, nor an increase in premiums. Years of motivational messages came flooding back to me. Norman Vincent Peale's famous line, "The only people with no problems are those in cemeteries," now took on a more poignant meaning. The time had come for me to see how intense my belief in myself was. There could be no room for doubt, no hesitation or uncertainty. Not achieving *this* goal meant not achieving any other goal—ever.

Bob Proctor, a motivational speaker, often came to mind during this trying period. I recalled two phrases that would give me the strength to ignore the dire prophecies of my caretakers: "If you can't see yourself doing something, you will never do it" and "We cannot outgrow the limits we impose on ourselves until we enlarge our image of ourselves." If my expectations were going to govern my life, I was going to aim high!

But I not only had to be determined to reach my goals, but I also had to ward off the negative anticipations of my doctors. Their desire to avoid fostering any false hope could have killed me. They meant to save me from disappointments. They knew the odds and tried to explain them to me. They wanted me to be realistic. I refused to accept *their* reality; I was going to create my own.

Zig Ziglar, the motivator who has inspired me more than any other, has a term for this situation, SNIOP'ed. It means to be "susceptible to the negative influence of other people." Studies show that other people's negative expectations often become self-fulfilling prophecies—teachers, bosses, spouses, parents, doctors—they can lock you in a cage of limits. If you accept these limits, you'll never go beyond them. But you have the key. Unlock the cage with self-confidence, and you can go as far as you desire.

I had unlocked the cage. It was now time to step out of it. With a blink of my eyes, I agreed to an operation never before performed, with a one in 1,000 chance of survival. Without it, according to the experts, I would be bedridden and would probably waste away and die. With the surgery, again according to the experts, if I lived through it, I might be able to sit in a wheelchair—someday. There was no hesitation when the doctor came for my approval. I told myself that I would fool everyone and come through it, ready to continue along the path of recovery.

No one else, except my mother-in-law, was that optimistic.

As they wheeled the stretcher from intensive care to the operating room, the hall was a gallery of loved ones. They all believed this was the last time they'd see me alive. My uncles, Pete and Sidney, went to pray for me. My wife stayed close to her parents. My mother-in-law kept telling everyone I would make it. But it seemed too impossible to believe.

The operation took close to nine hours. During that time, my torn and damaged neck ligaments were replaced with a special plastic material. My neck was fused from the first to the fourth cervical vertebrae (C-1 to C-4). Everything was held in place by wire. It was an incredible strain on my already over-taxed body, a trauma so severe that it would be a miracle if I lived.

When the doctors filed out of the operating room, they

did not see my wife's mother standing there. Wiping sweat from his brow, one doctor turned to a colleague and said, "I don't know how that guy is alive after what we did to him. I've never seen anything like that in my life."

I had beaten the odds.

Dr. Rish came out and told my family that I had made it through surgery. He emphasized that the next 48 hours would be critical. Whether or not I made it depended on how much fight I had in me. The odds of survival were still mighty slim.

And if I did pull through, what then? The outlook was bleak.

"If he survives, he will be paralyzed," explained Dr. Rish, "only able to blink his eyes the rest of his life. The most hope I can give you is that in 20 months he might, and I emphasize the word *might*, be able to sit in a wheelchair without being strapped in." A nursing home and a short, useless life seemed like certainties.

Once again, I was connected to benevolent monsters, the machines that kept vigil over me, performing life-giving functions. The loneliness I felt was worse than all the pain. Although I was only a few feet away from other patients and many nurses, I felt isolated, shut off from the outside world. Without the ability to communicate with others, I lacked the stimulation my brain needed so badly. It would have been easy to let my mind roam freely to create scenarios of fear and disaster. For some reason, negative and destructive thoughts multiply with little or no effort. It is the positive and constructive images that take an enormous amount of mental energy.

If I gave up, no one would fault me. I'd suffered so much; I had so little to live for. There would be a lifetime of anguish and humiliation. I would have less autonomy than a newborn infant. The strain on my family and friends would be tremendous.

But that wasn't the picture *I* saw. I believed with all my heart and soul that I would one day be normal: not hooked to machines, not silent, not fed through tubes, not pushed in a wheelchair, not institutionalized for the rest of my life. I was going to *live*. I knew it would be a long, hard struggle. I would have to rely on my own faith—no one else was crazy enough to even dream of Morris being a real person ever again.

I had overcome the odds before. My career attested to that

and so did my operation. From this time on, I would envision myself as *myself*, not the invalid everyone else saw. And I retold one story to myself, over and over, day in and day out. I'd heard Zig Ziglar recount a World War II tale in his speeches, and it gave me the courage to push on. The story went like this:

During a bloody campaign, General Creighton W. Abrams, Jr. was completely surrounded by the enemy. He called the members of his top staff together to brief them on the encirclement. Instead of taking a negative approach, the general announced, "We now have an opportunity that we have not had in this entire campaign. For the first time, we have the chance to attack the enemy from any direction."

Every damaged organ, broken bone, and unusable limb was my enemy. I could let them destroy me or I could undermine their overwhelming numbers by overcoming them, one at a time. And so, I began my fight for life.

chapter **2**

TO COMMUNICATE

Isolation is the worst possible counselor.

MIGUEL DE UNAMUNO

Finally, on March 17, the day arrived for my transfer from solitary confinement to the open area of the intensive care unit. Although I was in a private room for only seven days, it seemed like forever. I was joining nine other patients right in front of the nurses' station. Lights and activity, rather than a dark enclosed room, greeted me. Previously, it might have been two hours or more before I saw anyone. Now there were doctors and nurses everywhere. I couldn't communicate verbally, but I was beginning to feel in touch with my environment. The alienation I had felt was quickly replaced by a sense of warm human interaction.

The only movable limb I had, my right leg, became my means of calling for assistance. Then the nurses played a guessing game to find out what I needed. They asked me questions, and I replied by blinking: once for yes, twice for no. Most of the time, we succeeded, although it was usually a tiring, frustrating, time-consuming process. My sister and I had a much easier time of it; it was almost as if she could read my mind. With her M.A. in special education, Pat really undersood how draining this procedure was. She began work on a new system that would be simple enough to grasp quickly, yet detailed enough to discover my needs with a minimum of guesswork.

As my condition stabilized, I was allowed to have more visitors. The increasing need to communicate with these people, who sometimes traveled long distances to see me, made me eager to get the new system completed and into use.

When the code was ready that same St. Patrick's Day, it was an instant success. (See Appendix at the back of the book for code charts and keys.) First there was the *"Body Card"*: a large piece of cardboard with a sketch of a body, sectioned off and numbered. We used this to pinpoint any pain I needed to discuss. General questions, answerable by blinks for yes or no, narrowed the area down to front or back, or above or below the waist. Then we found the pain on the card by a process of elimination.

A second card was titled "Key Subject Areas," listing topics we needed to talk about frequently. There was also a "Persons Card" broken down into family, friends, and business or medical personnel, which had a companion card listing telephone numbers.

The "Alphabet Card" was the most important of them all. For the next three months, it was my link to the outside world. Unlike typical cards used in hospitals and rehabilitation centers, which list only two lines of letters, A through M and N through Z, my sister had divided her card into four sections. Each section contained two lines. Blinking to indicate the section I wanted, we could eliminate letters quickly, avoiding a letter-by-letter yes or no for half of the alphabet.

Once I was familiar with the breakdown of letters, I began to blink only when the right section was indicated. Then, whether my reply was yes or no, she could determine which of the two lines the letter was on. Soon we were able to find the letter on each section of the card by my staring at it, Pat following my gaze.

With ten minutes of practice, most people could "talk" with me easily. During my first week, Pat acted as interpreter for my evening visitors. After that, my friends, nurses, and doctors became familiar enough with the system to give a quick lesson to any newcomers.

One of my first callers, other than family members, was Doug Martin. He was the friend who'd intended to fly with me the day of my accident. As he entered the intensive care unit, he looked over the patients, trying to find me. But I was beyond recognition. My head had been shaved for my recent operation, my face and neck were swollen and twice their normal size, and my eyes were puffy and black.

"Where is Morris?" Doug asked. My appearance was quite a shock to him. I'm sure that thoughts of "what if" had crossed his mind many times since that fateful day.

After discussing my condition, we talked about my business. Doug assured me that he would do all he could to keep things going until I could get back on my feet. At the time of the accident, I'd had a number of cases still outstanding with

Union Mutual, a company Doug represented. His help would be invaluable in the coming months.

Because I was a broker for many companies and my clients were large corporations and wealthy people located in a number of states, keeping my finances in order would be a major problem. I had built a substantial, selective business in estate and tax planning over the past eight years. I had been bringing in a six-figure salary, with realistic expectations of reaching a half million per year within five years. Except for some moderate commissions, this expectation had come to a screeching halt because of the accident.

Another friend, Landon Browning, had been a former partner of mine. He knew more about my business than anyone else. So when he came for a visit, I turned over all my business dealings to him. He kept the wheels going when they threatened to jam irreparably.

Melvin Friedman, a prominent Virginia Beach attorney and a fishing partner of mine, also played a major role in reconstructing the shambles of my finances. I had not kept my wife, Sandy, informed about money and work matters. I now realized that she would be unable to stay afloat in our swiftly changing financial currents without someone throwing her a life preserver. With Sandy's agreement, I granted Mel power of attorney. He could act as an impartial third party and suggest the necessary decisions based on sound legal principles. This was a relief.

But there was still another major move to be made; there was an urgent need to file for bankruptcy. Mel understood. He must have been horrified after reviewing my financial records. Over the past several months, I had suffered heavy losses of hundreds of thousands speculating in gold and silver. To cover my commodity losses, I had borrowed heavily from several local banks. I had been forced to take second and third mortgages on my home. Things had reached the point where it took $7,500 a month to meet expenses. Even so, I had felt confident that I could work things out and repay my debts.

I had a good, solid earning capacity. Business was booming. I had several big deals in the works that would bring in a lot of money. But I couldn't kid myself any longer. Without me, the deals in progress would never be closed. They required specialized knowledge that only I possessed. They were based on trust and confidence between my clients and me. Delegating them to someone else was simply impossible.

Bankruptcy! It was almost unthinkable. All my life, I had prided myself on my excellent credit rating with many major lending institutions in the Tidewater area. I was able to borrow much more than my financial statement justified by simply signing my name. The bankers trusted me. They knew from past experience that if I promised to repay a loan by a certain time, I would. And in the past, I always had.

But things were different now. My main concern was the financial survival of my wife. Just a few months earlier, I had canceled a disability income policy that would have paid me $2,500 per month as long as I was disabled. I had planned on taking out a bigger and better policy, but had put off the medical exam. Now it was too late.

Luckily, I did have $1,600,000 of permanent life insurance. The premiums on these policies amounted to over $30,000 per year, but I had a disability waiver that meant that the insurance companies would pay the premiums for as long as I was disabled. The annual cash value buildup was over $30,000 per year. This would provide Sandy with a withdrawal amount of $2,500 per month for living expenses. However, this would not become effective until I had been disabled for six months.

In the meantime, I wanted Sandy to be secure. There was some money coming in from renewals on life insurance policies I had sold in the past. When an agent sells a policy, he gets paid a commission the first year and then a commission every year that the policy remains in force. So she did have some income. But upon declaring bankruptcy, all my renewals would go to the banks. If I had realized this at the time, I don't know if I could have withstood the stress.

And there was the accident itself. I needed to make sure that everyone understood that the crash was due to a mechanical failure, not to an error I had made. I communicated to Page Scott, who had witnessed the crash: "Crash not my fault—engine failed—held 2200 RPMs—fell to 800 RPMs—jammed full power—RPMs not increased." That brief explanation lifted a tremendous worry off my shoulders. Page said he understood and would look into the situation.

Time passes strangely in a hospital. Minutes seem like hours when there is no one to keep you company; when you are waiting on a rock-solid table for X-rays; when doctors and technicians are prodding swollen flesh to assess damages and healing; when nurses perform procedures so necessary yet so personal, like bathing and bowel stimulation.

Some days never seemed to end. I was in constant, excruciating pain. I slept infrequently and fitfully. At first, when I closed my eyes, I would relive the crash—the same picture over and over again. I saw the wires, then the nose of the plane meeting the ground, and then darkness. Or I saw the tunnel again—the light and the pictures of my life as vivid as the first time.

Once my condition was stabilized, these visions appeared less often. But then my sleep was interrupted by the hospital staff's routines. There was blood to be drawn, X-rays to be taken, sponge baths, sheet changes, rotation of my body to avoid bedsores. Night and day had no meaning. The only thing that mattered was the question, "How long until visiting hours?"

Every day, during afternoon and evening visiting hours, time raced by. The few hours I had to see my wife and other loved ones seemed compressed into seconds. There was usually a constant stream of people for me to see. Knowing that so many people cared about me was more helpful than any drug or treatment because it meant healing from within. It added to my inner strength, reinforcing my resolve to fight for life—for their sakes as well as mine.

My wife, Sandy, was there almost every day. On the days that she didn't come, I realized how much I needed her and how lost I would be without her. There was an emptiness that no one else could fill. A touch from her hand, the glow from her reassuring smile told me that we would conquer this adversity together.

I will never forget seeing my mother for the first time after the accident. She had a slight cold, so she came in wearing a surgical mask. The minute she saw me she began to cry. I had Pat tell her not to worry, that I would be okay. I blinked out, "I am tough; I will make it."

Then I asked her if she would promise me something. I told her that I wished she would stop smoking. Mother was a chain smoker, and I knew that she was killing herself a little more each day. If *I* was going to make it, I wanted *her* to make it, too. Before she left that day, she agreed to quit.

My wife's parents had been as close to me as any natural parents. When the others had held out little hope for my living through the operation, Mother Fink had assured them that I would pull through. She knew deep down that I was not a quitter. Yet the reality of my condition was difficult to bear. One evening, as my in-laws were preparing to leave, they cried. And I cried with them. We didn't weep out of pity or hopelessness or fear. We wept for love and hope and courage.

I did have some companions that didn't have to leave after visiting hours; my portable radio and my cassette tapes. The local radio station, WNIS, aired a talk show that I had always enjoyed. The sound of other people's voices was helpful in dispelling some of my loneliness. Without my glasses—they had been damaged in the accident and a replacement pair wasn't ready yet—the room and everyone in it were a blur. So the radio was also relaxing because I didn't have to strain to look at the speakers.

My music tapes were a big hit with the nurses. Kenny Rogers and John Denver seemed to be the favorites. It was great to sense the uplifted spirits of the staff as they hummed along while carrying out routine and sometimes distasteful procedures.

I also began listening to my motivational tapes: Zig Ziglar, Bob Proctor, Dr. Peale, and other speakers who had helped me through periods of self-examination and stress before. In my business, I couldn't show clients that I was having a bad day, and I couldn't retreat from the world under a pile of paperwork. It was certainly not a 9 to 5 job, either. Interacting with people, traveling frequently, and dealing with sums in the millions take their toll on even the most dedicated salesman. But I needed to project an image of energetic self-confidence to every customer. Would *you* entrust the stability of your company or the fate of your heirs to someone who had an exhausted appearance, a scowling face, or a flat, unexcited voice?

Listening to my tapes made me aware of how much more energy there is in all of us. We only need to discover how to release it. As Zig Ziglar says, "When you turn on a light switch, you don't create electrical power. You simply release the power that is there all the time." I believe there's a switch in all of us, a mental switch. People who have succeeded have learned how to flip that switch. I was determined to draw on all the power at my disposal so that I could succeed at becoming a normal human being again.

We take so much for granted in everyday life. How often have you complained about the time it takes to shave and shower? They seem like such mundane chores, nuisances. But when you can't do these tasks for yourself, and they're painful as well, you begin to appreciate how complicated these simple routines really are.

Each morning my sheets were changed, I was given a sponge bath, and I was shaved. Each of these activities required movement or pressure on my already aching body. Of them all, shaving was the worst.

Although my forehead was numb, every nerve ending in my face was alive, and my skin was hypersensitive. The slightest touch caused extreme pain. The inexpensive razors provided by the hospital and the use of soap instead of shaving lotion as a lubricant became unbearable. Meticulous, clean-cut Morris thought seriously about growing a beard. But Sandy didn't think much of the idea, so we tried my electric razor. That required too much rubbing and pressure. My sister bought some disposable razors and some shaving cream. They worked wonderfully. I still had to put up with the torture of being rolled from side to side for sheet changes and baths, but at least shaving was reduced to being a minor discomfort.

One morning, shortly after this cleansing ritual was completed, Dr. Rish came to check on me. I greeted him with a big smile, despite my discomfort.

"How do you feel today?" he wanted to know.

I blinked once to indicate I was okay. Then he asked me to follow a light with my eyes as he examined them. Propping a pillow on the left side of my face, he adjusted my neck.

Then he lit into the nurses. This situation was intolerable; my neck must be straight at all times, he told them.

Redirecting his attention back to me, the doctor said, "Try to wiggle your toes on your right foot." I tried, but couldn't.

"Now your left," he continued. Again it was impossible. With that, he left. And the nurses breathed a sigh of relief.

The hospital had an excellent nursing staff. But Dr. Rish had a reputation as being a perfectionist. All the nurses were apprehensive in his presence because they knew that if something had not been done to his exact specification, he would not hesitate to tell them about it. I must say that it was reassuring to know that I'd be taken care of properly, or else!

Next came the eyes, nose, and throat (ENT) specialists. They proceeded to examine my throat. After numbing the inside of my nose with cotton swabs soaked in an anesthetic, they inserted a long black tube into my right nostril. One end had a light, and the other had an eyepiece. In less than 30 seconds, the doctor withdrew the tube, saying that my throat was still too swollen for him to make an estimate of the damage. The swelling of my crushed larynx and voice box would have to be reduced before they could try again.

Several mornings later, I awoke with breathing difficulties. I was still completely dependent on a respirator, so this could be a life-threatening situation, I thought to myself. The ENT doctors were called in, and after a brief examination, they discovered that I had developed double pneumonia. Within a half hour, the respiratory team connected a machine that pumped medication into my lungs.

This procedure would help break up the congestion and kill the infection. They promised to check on me in a few hours.

Ten minutes later, Dr. Rish came in to tell me I'd be going down to get some X-rays soon. I was becoming so frustrated; he was ready to rush off again, and I needed to talk with him. There were so many things I wanted to say to him, and so many questions that I needed answered. I blinked my eyes rapidly to catch his attention.

"Is there something you need to tell me?" he asked. I wanted to shout out "Yes!" but could only blink once to say it.

Turning to the nurse, he asked, "Do you know how to communicate with him using his chart?" She said that she did.

"Okay, make it snappy," he ordered. As the nurse reached to get my chart, I realized that this was my big chance. But I knew he couldn't stay for long.

"Great doctor," I blinked out. Smiling, the nurse turned to Dr. Rish and conveyed the message. A friendly grin crossed his face. As he turned to leave, he told me that he was going to take really good care of me. Motivation is a two-way street.

After he'd gone, the nurse told me that I had accomplished more with two words than the entire nursing staff had been able to do in three years. From that moment on, Dr. Rish and I had a relationship that transcended the usual doctor-patient bond. I had gotten through to him.

Too soon, it was time for the X-rays.

"You're not scared, are you?" asked Dr. Rish.

I blinked twice, but deep down I was frightened. What would they find out? They wheeled me into the X-ray department and said they would get to me quickly. Fifteen minutes later, Dr. Rish appeared with flames in his eyes. He wanted to know why I was not on the table and ready to go. Suddenly the whole department came alive.

"Just hang in there, and we'll have you back to your room before you know it," he reassured me.

First, Dr. Rish and a radiologist examined my diaphragm. It was not functioning. This meant that I could not breathe on my own.

Next, they checked my swallowing reflex. I was asked to "open wide" but my jaw was so severely crushed that I could barely move it enough to allow a thin syringe to be placed in the back of my throat. They squirted some dye into my mouth for me to swallow. I tried several times, but it just didn't work. The results of these tests confirmed my worst suspicions. It was going to be harder than I thought, but I was still sure I could overcome every obstacle.

"That's all for today," the nurse told me. I was wheeled back to my room. Thank goodness it was almost time for visiting hours.

"How are you doing, sport?" It was the voice of Dr. Leonard Oden, a dear friend who'd shared many happy days of hunting and fishing with me. I'd first met him at the age of 13 when he straightened my teeth. Then, after my father died— I was only 17—we became as close as any father and son could be. He had five daughters and no sons, so we each filled a void in the other's life.

Len had never been at a loss for words, but the sight of me left him speechless. He stared at me as if in a stupor. A nurse broke the unnerving silence by explaining to him how he could use the charts to communicate with me. We were soon reliving old times, enjoying once again wonderful days of out-door adventure and togetherness. These memories helped me visualize how I would be one day in the future—able to stomp through swamps, shoulder a gun, ride a boat, reel in a prize fish. Such is the curative power of communication between friends. Before Len left, I indicated to him that there was some-one I needed to contact, someone who might be able to speed up my recovery.

Dr. C. Curtis Shears, head of the Nutritional Science Re-search Institute of England in Gloucester, had been longtime friends with Dr. Oden. The three of us had gone on many fishing trips together during the week or two he would come to visit Len each year. I'd always picked his brain, trying to get as much information out of this incredible man as I possibly could. Although almost 80 years old, Dr. Shears got along like a 40-year-old. He told me once that he would live to be 150, and I believed him.

Through his work at the institute, Dr. Shears, along with fellow nutritionists in the United States, can analyze an indi-vidual's body balance of vitamins and minerals, using a hair sample. After determining any deficiencies or excesses, a chart of the most harmful and beneficial foods for that person can be prepared.

I had been having my hair analyzed every six months and adjusting my diet as it became necessary. I really believe that my survival during the critical phase after the crash was due to having maintained a proper nutritional balance for so many years.

But now, all I was receiving was a glucose drip—sugar water. I needed an expert to get my body chemistry back in shape for the strenuous task of recovery.

Len had not been gone more than 30 minutes when a respiratory therapist arrived to start my lung treatments. Pneu-monia had taken such a hold on me that my breathing was becoming very shallow. A deep breath created a searing pain in my chest. Rolling me on my left side, the therapist began pounding on the right side of my ribs with his fists! This was incredibly painful and seemed almost medieval. But the mucus in my lungs had to be loosened and removed or I would drown in my own fluids.

After about 15 minutes, I was rolled onto my right side,

and the whole process was repeated. Then the plug to my tracheotomy was removed and a thick black tube inserted through the hole in my throat all the way into my lungs. There was an air bag shaped like a football on the end of the tube. By squeezing it, the therapist forced air into my lungs to help break up more of the accumulated mucus.

This tube was removed and replaced by another. The second tube was hooked up to a machine that acted like a vacuum cleaner, which sucked up all the loose mucus. The tube was transparent. I watched in awe as a thick yellow substance filled the tube. With this graphic proof of the need for treatment, the pain of therapy became more bearable.

Nevertheless, it came as a shock to learn that this procedure had to be performed every four hours. It was to take four months of treatments and many operations before my lungs would be clear again.

During this draining period, I did not give up hope. In fact, a friend who'd been my guest for a goose hunt just that November, Verlin Griffin, came to visit one day. I blinked a message to Pat for him: "I'll come down in November and go deer hunting with you." Verlin just smiled. Nobody thought that I'd even live, much less go deer hunting. But the pictures of me hunting and fishing gave me the strength and courage to go forward. I was sure that I'd be an outdoorsman again.

The doctors, however, said that due to the extensive nerve damage I had sustained, my diaphragm would never work again. Even if the pneumonia were cured, I would be on a respirator for the rest of my life. That was not for me.

I closed my eyes and tried to sort out all my problems and place them in order of importance. After hours of deep thought, I decided that being able to breathe on my own had to be my number one goal. I couldn't think of being active again until I was set free of this machine.

chapter 3

TO BREATHE

They say you treat people exactly as you see them. I wanted people to see me not as a hopeless vegetable, but as a man who would one day stand tall again.

MORRIS GOODMAN

As a young boy, I loved to walk through the woods hunting squirrel. My uncle had a farm in the country, so I spent all my free time there. I remember a ridge covered with hardwood trees: hickory, maple, chestnut, and oak. My uncle told me that some of them were 200 years old. I would pick up acorns and examine them in wonder as I thought about how these huge trees had sprouted from such a tiny beginning.

Many years later, I saw an inspiring message in this. To become a giant oak, an acorn had to be planted in the darkness of the earth, nourished by the earth and sky, and then it would emerge one day as a tiny plant. This small seedling had to weather many storms, yet it grew stronger as it survived these trials.

Like the young oak tree, I would have to weather many storms in the months and years ahead. And I would grow stronger as I survived one, and then another storm, each preparing me for the next. One day I would stand as tall and triumphant as those giant oaks.

Once again, the respiratory team came to pound on my chest, or so I thought. Instead, they wheeled in a strange-looking gadget and plugged it in. I was told that it was a large vibrator, to be used on my chest and rib cage to break up the congestion. The discomfort of this new treatment was amazingly small, although the suctioning of loose mucus was still extremely painful.

Why haven't they been using the vibrator all along, I wondered. Maybe it isn't as effective in breaking up the mucus, or there's some other reason, I thought. I did not find out the reason until much later. The hospital had only one vibrator. If it was available when the time came for your treatment, it was used. But there were many other patients who needed this piece of equipment. It was disturbing to think about the suffering caused by the lack of a vital machine in this multimillion dollar medical complex. I promised myself that someday I would donate one or two vibrators and save future patients from unnecessary torture.

The respiratory team left, and I indicated to the nurse that I would like to listen to the radio. For the next two hours, I lost myself in the action of a University of Virginia versus Maryland basketball game, temporarily escaping the reality of my present condition.

When the game ended, I once more focused on my situation. After about an hour, a thought came to me—a powerful thought that would not go away. It was like a voice deep within my mind that kept repeating "breathe deep, breathe deep." At the time, I was still hooked up to the respirator, which was doing my breathing for me. But my respiration was very shallow.

I soon found that I could breathe with the respirator. This meant trying to inhale a little air and expanding my lungs as much as I could. My chest ached, but I continued. After 100 breaths, I stopped to see if my lungs would expand on their own. Nothing happened. Yet the voice kept saying, "You must keep trying."

All night long I stayed awake, repeating the process: 100 deep breaths, a five-minute rest, another 100 breaths, another brief rest.

When morning arrived, I was still practicing. I was not tired, but the pain in my chest had become severe. Convinced that I was doing something that would help me to recover, I knew that I must continue to bear it. It was as if God were speaking to me, and I had no right to question His judgment.

My faith never wavered. Despite seemingly insurmountable odds, I refused to think of quitting. As far as I knew, no one had ever tried this, let alone succeeded. I had no indication that it was doing any good. But I had an abundance of time and a burning desire to overcome my dependency on the respirator. A seedling had been planted in my mind, and it would require time and a lot of tender care before it began to bear fruit. Until then, it had to be nurtured and guarded so that the winds of hopelessness did not uproot it. I didn't tell the doctors of my breathing plan. They would probably have told me that I was being completely unrealistic; I wasn't about to let them trample my seedling and then wonder why it had died.

That same morning, March 21, an unfamiliar nurse entered my room. The respiratory team had decided that I needed a bronchoscopy, she said, and she had come to get my approval. They also needed my wife's okay, so the necessary papers would be prepared and waiting for her when she arrived for visiting hours.

"Would you like to know what a bronchoscopy is?" the nurse asked.

Well, maybe some people don't care to hear about what will be done to them, or they unquestioningly trust their doctors. And maybe she would have explained the procedure anyway and just asked the question out of habit. But I was determined to understand what this operation was all about before I agreed to anything.

Basically, it was a procedure to help remove mucus from my lungs, the nurse explained. First, my tracheotomy plug would be removed. Then, my throat would be anesthetized. Next, a pencil-thin tube with a lighted end and a magnifying eyepiece on the other end would be inserted into my lungs. The surgeon would try to remove as much mucus as he could see. I was told that there would be only minor discomfort, a falsehood that I would discover all too soon. But I could not have avoided the surgery. My life depended on it.

As I watched the nurses scurrying around, preparing me for the operation, I thought back to how busy I had been before the crash. What a contrast there was between the supercharged bundle of energy and enthusiasm I had been and the immobile prisoner I was now.

I also recalled a saying by Bob Proctor: "What is a man but his mind? Everything else you can find on a donkey or a cow." As I looked around the room, I realized that everything in the room—the bed, the clock, the windows, the medical tools and machines—had once been just an idea in someone's mind. If the mind were powerful enough to accomplish all this, I felt certain that it could provide solutions to my problems.

And then I thought of Thomas Edison. On one of his tapes, Zig Ziglar relates a story about the young Edison and his refusal to give up. This diligent inventor had worked for years on the incandescent light bulb. After over 10,000 tries, a young reporter asked how it felt to have failed 10,000 times. Edison retorted: "You and I look at things differently. You see, the way I look at it, I have not failed 10,000 times. I have successfully found 10,000 things that will not work." It took over 4,000 more experiments before he found a combination that did work.

We are indebted to Edison for his marvelous invention. But we may never have had this ingenious creation if it weren't for this man's positive thinking, persistence, and faith. Each time I looked at the lights in the ceiling, my resolve hardened. I would give my life as much of a chance as Edison had given his light bulb.

"You aren't worried, are you?" asked Sandy, when she arrived at 2:00 P.M.

I blinked twice to indicate that I was not, but my eyes must have betrayed me. In order to continue my plan for recovery, I had to live through this operation, and each surgical procedure placed a heavy drain on my system.

"I spoke to the nurse, and she said it was a simple procedure. She said there was nothing to worry about," Sandy said, trying to reassure me. But these words had been spoken so many times during the past few days that I was becoming numb to them.

Sandy left to sign the consent forms. When she returned—in 15 minutes that seemed like forever—she told me that everything was ready and that she would stay until the surgery was over to make sure I was all right.

Almost immediately, two nurses dressed in surgical green came in. One of them was the woman who'd explained the procedure to me, and she said, "You just relax and leave everything to us. We'll take good care of you."

In a few minutes, two doctors appeared dressed for surgery.

"We are ready to begin," one of them said. "I'll try to be as gentle as I can."

I began to panic. Surely they aren't going to operate on me right here, I thought. Well, that's what they intended to do. The younger doctor, perhaps an intern or a student, began to remove my tracheotomy tube. Then a syringe was inserted into my throat to numb my lungs. I felt a cold sensation ease along my throat down into my chest.

Next, the other doctor began to insert a thin black tube into my lungs. It was similar to the instrument I had seen a few days earlier when they had examined my throat. This tube enabled the doctor to reach places in my lungs that weren't accessible by normal suction techniques.

"You did just fine," said the doctor. "We got a lot of stuff out of there, and I am well pleased. You just close your eyes and rest for a while, and I will check on you later."

They gathered all their tools, and, like a band of gypsies slipping away in the middle of the night, they were gone.

The pain did not go away. As the medication wore off, my chest felt as if someone had poured gasoline down my throat and had lit it. Was this the "minor discomfort" the nurses had soothed me with? How much more would I have to endure?

As evening visiting hours approached, I tried to close my eyes and rest. But inactivity was more difficult to deal with than exertion. I began my breathing exercises again. The pain was overwhelming, and I had to stop—for the time being. I'll try again later tonight, I said to myself. No matter how long it takes, I will overcome all my disabilities and be whole once more.

I knew how important it was to keep all negative thoughts out of my mind. It would have been easy to commit mental suicide. A story I had once read reminded me of how vital our perception of a situation can be, sometimes more important than reality. I was thinking of a story by a psychologist, Dr. Dudley Calvert, as told by Dr. Harold R. McAlingdon. The tale describes the fate of a middle-aged man working on a railroad in Russia. By accident, he locked himself into a refrigerator car. He banged on the door, he screamed, but no one heard him. Finally, he accepted his destiny. He sat down. His body became numb. With his fingers, he scribbled a message on the wall to those who would eventually find him.

"I'm becoming colder now. Starting to shiver. Nothing to do but wait. I am slowly freezing to death. Half asleep now. I can hardly write. These may be my last words."

They were. Five hours later, the door was opened and the man was found dead. A sad story—but there's a twist.

The temperature inside the car was 56 °. The refrigeration unit was broken, and there was sufficient oxygen to breathe. He had willed himself to die. He was so certain he would freeze to death, that he did.

If the mind has so much destructive power, surely it has the potential for healing power as well. I was determined to concentrate all my efforts toward breathing on my own. I had already achieved my first goal—life. With my sister's help, I had made contact with my environment. I was progressing faster than anyone had thought possible. But I had to be on guard constantly. My enemies—exhaustion, pain, and fear— were always waiting for an opportunity to undermine my self-confidence and my health.

There is an ancient fable about the Devil's sale that I once heard Earl Nightingale tell. Satan was having a sale of his wares. Everything was prominently displayed and marked with a price— the rapier of jealousy, the dagger of fear, the strangling noose of hatred. Separate, and elevated on a purple pedestal, was the wedge of discouragement. It was not for sale at any price. The Devil could stay in business without the others, but he couldn't win souls without his wedge.

Discouragement can take over a person's soul. It can eat away his hope and self-confidence with doubts and self-pity, leaving an empty, useless shell. Yes, I was battling some powerful enemies, but knew that if I pooled all my inner resources, I could survive the onslaught.

That evening was the first time I could remember not being in the mood to see anyone during visiting hours. My lungs and chest were very sore, and I was incredibly tired. But I greeted my sister with a forced smile.

"How are you feeling tonight?" she asked.

Lying, I blinked a yes to her.

It was a busy night. When my friends and family left, the quiet presented a perfect atmosphere for the noxious fumes of negative thoughts to invade my mind. But I refused to succumb to them.

I must rid myself of this respirator, I kept repeating. Every time the respirator took a breath for me, I tried to inhale deeply. For hours I would persistently practice. According to modern medicine, my goal was unattainable. But I continued.

At least I didn't have to be concerned with other people's opinions. No one else knew of my grueling program. If they had, they may have talked me out of it. Of course, they'd have meant well, but without a 100 percent commitment, I'm not sure that I could have sustained the belief that I really could succeed.

For the first time in many days, I'd begun to feel tired; not the fatigue resulting from mental and physical stress, but a yearning for sleep. The hospital routines continued, however: respiratory therapy every four hours, around the clock, constant administering of medicine and changing of IV tubes. I was still awake the morning of March 22, yet I kept my eyes closed, hoping sleep would come.

Suddenly, I had an overwhelming feeling that someone was staring at me. I immediately opened my eyes, and there stood my old friend, Dr. Eugene Poutasse, a brilliant kidney surgeon.

"Do you know who this is?" he asked, and I indicated that I did.

At the time, I was catheterized to aid in urinating. Dr. Poutasse asked if it was uncomfortable, and I blinked that it was.

He decided that I'd do without it for a day and see how it went. That was the best news I'd had since my move from isolation to the nurses' station two weeks ago. A huge grin showed him how pleased I was. Once the catheter was removed, a condom was attached to a collection bag and hung at the bottom of the bed. I never needed to be catherized again. This was a major hurdle for me. It seemed as though I was finally improving, however slowly.

Soon I experienced another first. A woman appeared, wearing a uniform slightly different from those the nurses wore.

"I'm your physical therapist, and I will be working with you every day," she explained. "Are you ready to get started?"

I couldn't have been readier. She started to move my arms. Then she worked on my legs. As she proceeded, she explained that this was called ranging—trying to maintain or increase the range of movement in my limbs by rotating and bending them. Until I regained enough control to move them myself, this activity would keep my joints from becoming stiff. She encouraged me to exercise my right leg, as I already had some control of movement in it. Although there was some movement in my left leg, it was difficult to tell if muscle reflexes or spasticity—involuntary contractions—was the cause. She would pick up my legs, one at a time, and ask me to push down, but there was no response.

Bending my right leg back toward my chest, she asked me to kick toward her. I concentrated intently. I think I caught her by surprise when I actually pushed her hand forward. It was only a slight movement, but to me it was a milestone.

The doctors still warned my family not to get their hopes up. They believed that my chances of ever walking again were one in a million. Dr. Rish told my wife that if I ever learned to sit in a wheelchair without being strapped in, it would be a miracle—I had no sense of balance and probably never would.

I'll show you all, I said to myself. I saw myself as a man walking tall and straight. As soon as I was free of the respirator, I would work on my other goals, and walking on my own two feet was one of them.

The morning had passed quickly, thanks to Dr. Poutasse, the physical therapist, and a Zig Ziglar tape. It was already time for visiting hours. My sister arrived, and so did Landon Browning, my former business partner.

"I've got some things to go over with you. Do you feel up to it?" he asked. I felt as if I could handle just about anything at that moment, so we discussed the questions Landon had brought with him. Many of them only required a yes or no. Those that needed a longer answer were resolved by using Pat as an interpreter. We covered a lot of ground, but I was worn out from the strain.

Pat and Landon left, and the respiratory team arrived. One day all of this would be over. For now, though, I had to take one day at a time.

That evening was fairly quiet. Only a few relatives came to visit, and I spent the rest of the night listening to my radio and practicing my breathing. The radio was tuned to a local country music station, WCMS. Everything was peaceful and relaxing until a nurse came over and changed the station to a teenage rock and roll program.

She hadn't even bothered to ask me if it was okay! Before

I could get her attention, she was gone. I was so mad, I thought I'd explode. Then there was a comical turn of events. A distinguished doctor walked over and looked at me.

"Morris, don't you think you're a little old for this kind of music?" I laughed at the irony of the situation. The radio station was eventually tuned back to my original station. Some time after midnight, I finally drifted off to sleep—the first time in almost a week.

When I awoke the next morning, I felt refreshed and full of energy. I was ready to meet any challenge.

All my life, I've had a strong desire to win at whatever I did. Many of my friends had referred to it as a killer instinct. Being second isn't enough—I must be first.

It is the kind of burning desire that triggers the extra energy anyone needs to achieve a goal. When we are bubbling over with enthusiasm, obsessed with an aim, anything is possible.

I resumed my breathing exercises with a new vigor. I increased the number of breaths before a rest from 100 to 200. I practiced for several hours, with no results. But I wouldn't give up. It was a matter of survival for my doctors, my friends, and my family to see me as a person, not as a vegetable. I had to reach my goals myself, yet their support and genuine belief that I would succeed would help me get through the rough times.

Sandy arrived at noon while the physical therapist was working on me. The therapist showed Sandy how to range my arms and legs so that she could exercise me between scheduled therapy sessions. At first my wife was timid. Maybe she was afraid she'd hurt me. Soon she was working with me like a pro.

"I spoke with Dr. Rish yesterday for about two hours," she began as soon as the therapist left. "That's why I wasn't here. He wants to send you to Charlottesville for more advanced treatment." She went on to tell me that the University of Virginia Hospital there had a reputation as one of the top spinal cord facilities in the United States.

"There is a place called The Towers, where they take you swimming, bowling, rifle shooting, and all sorts of things." She was trying to make it sound exciting. The more she talked, the easier it was to accept. No date had been set yet, she said, but it would be soon.

What bothered me about this new place was the distance. It must be 250 miles away, I thought. I would be isolated from my friends and family. Although I tried to convince myself that they would come to visit me often, I had my doubts. And I'd have to adjust to a new hospital staff.

As the time grew closer to the move, Dr. Rish came in often to explain things to me concerning the changeover. I started looking forward to the trip. I was ready to devote more time to my recovery so that I could return to a normal life again.

One afternoon I had my sister give a message to Dr. Rish. "I will return in four months. I will walk into your office and shake your hand." He just smiled. I'm sure he thought it would be miraculous if in two years I rolled into his office in a wheelchair.

It was April Fools' Day. I had been keeping up with the date by following a calendar that hung from my bed. About 11:00 that morning, my physical therapist came in.

"How are you feeling today?" she asked. I looked at her with a worried expression and blinked twice. That caught her attention. Good old Morris always had a smile on his face.

"Is there something the matter?" she wanted to know. I blinked my eyes one time. She reached for the Alphabet Card. The message I gave was: "Can't move right leg—get doctor now."

Dropping the card, she raced to the nurses' station to summon help. Almost immediately, there were two more nurses at my bedside.

"What seems to be the problem, Morris?" they inquired worriedly. "Just spell it out." I blinked back the words, "April Fools." Then I grinned as widely as I could.

Well, they all laughed. But I had a feeling that they could just as easily have killed me for giving them such a scare!

The date for my move was finally set: April 6, a Monday. I would be moved by ambulance. Sandy would ride with me, and her parents would follow us so that they could help me get settled. It seems as though everyone came to visit that Saturday and Sunday to wish me well before I left. By Sunday night, I was so exhausted I was sure I'd get a good night's sleep. But rather than sleeping late, I was wide awake at 6:00. It would be another hour before the nurse came to begin the preparations for my trip. But I could not rest, so I practiced my breathing and told myself that if I stopped now, I would have to start all over again.

Between 8:00 and 9:00, the area I had called home for the last few weeks changed from a place full of personal touches and reminders of everyone's moral support to a sterile hospital bed and table. The nurses on duty all came to say goodbye, but Dr. Rish was not around. Perhaps he was tied up in surgery. At 9:00, the ambulance arrived, and I was loaded into the vehicle—tubes, wires, and all. There had been many friends lining the hall as I was wheeled out, but one face struck me: my dear friend, Leonard Oden, was there to see me off even though he must have had to cancel or rearrange his own patients' appointments in order to be there.

Sometimes the inner strength gained from knowing that someone cares has a healing capacity far beyond the scope of modern medicine. As I was wheeled outside into the bright sunshine—the first time in three weeks—everything looked beautiful to me.

Once we got going, the paramedic sitting in the back with Sandy and me quickly caught on to the Alphabet Card. Sandy suggested that he ask me whether I would like to listen to any of my tapes. When he came to one by John Denver, I blinked once.

"I like John Denver also," he said. I began blinking my eyes rapidly. "Is something wrong?" he asked. Sandy told him that I wanted to tell him something.

"I used to be a top-notch guitarist," I began. I told him that I used to give concerts, playing mostly folk and country music.

The mellow sound of the music filled the back of the ambulance as I saw the interstate unfurling behind us like a black hair ribbon. The road—unwinding at 90 mph—had a hypnotic effect, and soon I was sound asleep.

When I awoke about an hour later, we were 15 miles south of Richmond. Sandy told me that we were going to be stopping for gas soon. After we had pulled into a station, Sandy's father asked me if he could get me something to drink. Yes, I blinked. "How would you like a nice cold Mountain Dew?" Sandy asked. Oh, boy, would I, I wanted to shout. That would be my first thing to drink since the accident.

Sandy returned with the drink and a straw. I could open my mouth just enough for her to get the straw between my lips. Because I still couldn't swallow, she let only a trickle run into my mouth, just to moisten and cool off my mouth. There was nothing wrong with my taste buds! It was just wonderful. But the sight of everyone else eating solid food—and the smell— was driving me crazy.

Soon we were off again, heading for the Blue Ridge Mountains and a new phase of my life. Only 27 days after my accident, I felt strange. It was as if I were leaving the old Morris behind and taking the new Morris with me. I knew that there was no way anyone, not even Sandy, could understand how I felt. In *To Kill a Mockingbird,* Atticus Finch tells his daughter, Scout, "You never really understand a person until you climb into his skin and walk around in it." God forbid anyone should have to get inside of me right now! That would have been cruel and unusual punishment. But I did wish someone could really empathize with me.

As we entered the beautiful college town of Charlottesville, I was glad to have reached our destination. The four-hour trip was very tiring, and I was eager to get on with the process of settling in.

"It's huge," exclaimed Sandy as we backed up to the emergency room doors. Everything was well organized, and I was whisked off to the fifth floor north wing and into a four-bed room.

Once all my things were arranged, my mother-in-law, father-in-law and Sandy left, saying they'd return after supper. They promised that they would stay for the next night or two until I was comfortable in my new surroundings.

It wasn't long before Dr. Richard Whitehill came by to say hello and to introduce himself as the doctor in charge of my case. He was an orthopedic surgeon and a professor at the University Medical School. His specialty was spinal cord problems associated with the back and neck. I had been told that he was the second best in the field in the *world.* That's quite an impressive reputation, and I was fortunate to be in such capable hands. My only complaint was that he was just too quick. Trying to get his attention, especially in my silent, immobile condition, was difficult to the point of frustration.

I soon found that there was another problem here. There was a nursing shortage. Instead of being in an open area under constant surveillance by most of the nursing staff, I was in a room with three other patients. This room was serviced by one nurse, who had two to four other rooms under her responsibility as well. That meant that in an hour's time, there was a nurse available to me for about ten minutes. And because I could not tell the nurses what I needed, I sometimes missed them completely and had to wait another hour to get their attention. I knew that we'd have to find a solution to this problem if I were to get the help I needed for my recovery.

When everyone had left for the evening, it was time for me to get back to the serious work of breathing. I was still taking 200 breaths and then resting for a few minutes. There was no indication that what I was doing would improve my condition, but the voice was always there reminding me to keep trying. I guess most people would have given up by then. They would have told themselves to be practical. Well, I had a dream, and dreams are not known for their practicality. If I quit, I had no chance for reaching my dream—so on I went.

April 7, my first morning at the new hospital, was not very different from Norfolk General. That didn't make the old routines easier to handle, though.

"I'll try not to hurt you," said a young woman who had come to draw some blood. You can't hurt me, I said to myself. After what I've been through, it'll take more than that little needle! I had had so much blood drawn during the past three weeks that my veins would not stand up. Every time a needle was inserted, they collapsed. This time it took four attempts before the woman got a sample.

Not ten minutes later, two doctors appeared. They examined my lungs and told me that the respiratory team would soon be in to treat me. In addition to the regular regimen every four hours, they were going to hook me to a machine that would constantly put moisture into my lungs. Medication would be added to this moisture every four hours.

The machine providing the moist air was wheeled into my

room, a clear hose was connected to my tracheotomy tube, and when the doctors were satisfied that everything was functioning properly, they left.

I hardly had time to relax before a nurse came to tell me that some chest X-rays were scheduled. I sure hope every day isn't this hectic, I thought to myself. I was dreading the transfer to a stretcher and the trip down to the lab. But I was pleasantly surprised. A portable X-ray machine was rolled right into my room, and the work was done without moving me from the bed.

After the X-ray technicians had left, I settled back to watch television. Each black-and-white set was shared by two patients, and each bed had a remote control box. I couldn't move my fingers or hands, so I'd have to watch whatever my neighbor chose. But for now, that didn't matter. It had been three weeks since I'd had a chance to see what was going on in the outside world.

Sandy and her mother and dad returned around noon and stayed until 2:00. Now came the hard part. It was time for them to leave.

"I'll be back in a few weeks," Sandy told me. Her parents also promised to return as soon as they could.

After they left, I felt an emptiness inside that was overpowering. Their intentions were good, but I knew that it would seem like forever between visits. Instead of 20 miles, I was 250 miles from all of my loved ones. For the second time, I broke down and cried.

For the next week and a half, I had to adjust to a new schedule. Each morning I would wake up at 6:30. Between 7:00 and 7:30, my doctors would visit to check on my progress. As soon as they left, it was time for my respiratory therapy. Then a nurse came to take a blood sample.

I remember one time when a young trainee tried 16 times to get blood. My arms felt like pincushions. Finally, out of desperation, she left to get help. A doctor came and had to draw the blood from my foot.

After the blood sample was taken, a nurse would bathe and shave me, and change the sheets.

Then I was weighed. The doctors kept a close watch on me, even though my weight changed by only an ounce every few weeks. Every morning two men would roll a flat scale next to my bed. It looked like a stretcher, and the flat platform could be raised, lowered, and extended sideways electrically. A nurse would lift me, then the platform was slid under me. Then I was forklifted off the bed to register my weight.

Next I was visited by the X-ray technicians. I've had so many X-rays, you could locate me with a Geiger counter!

Usually by 11:00, all of this was done, and I had about an hour to rest before the respiratory team came for another treatment.

Thank goodness the afternoons weren't as hectic. Sometimes there were more X-rays taken or more blood was drawn. But on most days, things were fairly quiet. Visiting hours were from noon until 2:00—a sad time, when everyone was far away. After a visit from one of my pulmonary doctors to check on my lungs and another respiratory treatment at 4:00, the afternoon was over.

Evenings were a time of relaxation. There were no evening visiting hours, so the ward was relatively inactive. I'd listen to tapes, watch TV, and listen to the other patients talking to each other. Even though I could not join in the conversations, I enjoyed listening to find out more about my roommates.

Friendships that I developed during my two-month stay in the University Hospital are still strong today. We all shared a common bond. We had been reduced from normal, functioning human beings to paper shells of our former selves. Some patients, like a 16-year-old boy who shared my room, would recover and return to an active life—he'd been in a car wreck and both legs had been broken but his back or spinal cord had not been damaged. Other patients had to face a life of paralysis because their spinal cords had been too severely damaged. And some had extensive damage but could still hope to regain mobility through therapy and sheer determination. I was sure that I was in this last category. The doctors believed that I would remain paralyzed.

Tom Elridge occupied a bed on the other side of the room. He was about 27 and was from Chesapeake, Virginia—a place not far from my home. Tom had been shot in the back with a pistol, and the bullet had lodged against his spinal cord. Fearing to do further damage, the doctors had decided to leave the bullet in. The pain Tom suffered was evidenced in his face and by his moans, despite injections of morphine every four hours.

I could empathize with Tom. I suffered from excruciating pain everywhere—legs, feet, stomach, neck, head, arms, jaw, buttocks—all were so sensitive that the slightest touch put me in agony. Yet I refused to take painkillers because I didn't want to become dependent on them or to be lulled into acceptance of my condition.

I looked at the positive side of the situation. As long as there was pain, there was feeling. Pain meant healing. If I had felt nothing, if all my nerves had been severed, there would have been no chance for recovery.

The contrast between my appearance and the mental image I had of myself is well illustrated by an incident that happened during the second day of my stay in Charlottesville. John Cordle, a man in his fifties, was admitted to my room. He was from Richlands, Virginia, a coal-mining community about 300 miles away. John had broken his back while cutting firewood— a tree had fallen on him.

John was visiting with his wife and two of his sons. They began discussing deer hunting, and I became excited. Blinking my eyes rapidly to get a nurse's attention, I hoped to communicate my enthusiasm to John. A nurse who was familiar with my Alphabet Card helped me ask John what his name was, but he didn't respond. He just ignored me. The nurse told me his name and left.

Several months later, I learned that John had told his wife that it was useless to tell me his name. "That man will be dead by morning," he had said. Well, I wasn't ready for the undertaker yet, but I guess I looked as if I were going to go any minute!

Unable to have a dialog with John, I retreated into my memory, recalling an outing I had gone on to hunt bobwhite quail when I was 18. It had been a bitterly cold day in mid-December, a cloudy day that threatened snow. I had been hunting, alone except for my dogs, Mutt and Prince, since daybreak. So far I'd gotten only about four birds. Then it began to snow. It was late afternoon and time to head back, but the dogs picked up on a covey of quail. I shot three on the rise, and the rest scattered in a fairly open area of woods.

It was an ideal place for Mutt and Prince to follow up on the single birds. The only thing that stood in our way was a swamp about 100 yards wide. Although the water was 8 to 15 feet deep and ice cold, I was sure that I could get across by walking along some fallen trees.

Holding my gun in front of me for balance, I started across. My boots were wet and the logs were covered with mud and snow, so I took great care with each step. Weighted down with heavy hunting clothes and boots, I would probably have drowned—if I didn't freeze to death first—if I slipped.

Halfway across the swamp, I looked down to see Prince swimming along beside me, but Mutt was nowhere in sight. Glancing over my shoulder, I watched in horror as he suddenly appeared, heading toward me on a collision course. As Mutt ran into me I lost my balance and I went overboard.

The water froze onto my face the minute I came to the surface. I dove back down several times before I found my gun. I could easily have shot that dog, but he had enough sense to stay away. Once I had pulled myself out and caught my breath, I began the seven-mile hike back to the farmhouse, shivering as I trudged through the woods in the swiftly enveloping darkness.

My boots had to be pounded with a hammer to break the ice surrounding my feet. I didn't lose any toes to frostbite, but it took almost 15 months before normal feeling returned to them.

Did I let this harrowing experience scare me away from a sport I loved? Certainly not! Episodes such as this are just a part of the game.

Slipping back into the present, I realized that I couldn't let my accident take away the outdoor life I had thrived on for so many years. Not only was I going to be able to function normally again, but I was also going to hunt and fish and enjoy life.

On Saturday, April 18, I had a surprise visit from Pat and Sandy. I had expected to have a sad and lonely Easter, but their presence and the white stuffed bunny they brought were great morale boosters.

We had so much catching up to do that for three hours we rambled on and on about what had happened over the last two weeks. One of my main concerns was the nursing situation. I needed to impress upon them how serious the shortage was. The nurses really tried, but sometimes I did not see a nurse for two hours, and then when one could get to me, there was not enough time to do everything.

I suggested that they look into getting me a private nurse. Landon could see if my insurance would cover the cost. Even if it wasn't covered, I felt that this was vital to my recovery.

Pat checked with the head nurse and got an okay and the names of several agencies in the area. Sandy promised me she'd check on the insurance as soon as she got home. Still, I didn't think that they understood the severity of the situation. I was isolated and helpless. And it was affecting my physical well-being as well as my mental state.

For the previous three hours, I had lived in the past and in the future. When they left, I was once again stuck in the present.

That night I was assigned a new nurse. His name was Randy Amos. At first I wasn't sure what to expect from such an unconventional staffer. But he soon proved to be completely competent. And there was a bonus. One of the pictures on my wall caught his eye, and he asked if that was me—it was a shot of me beaming from ear to ear, holding a beautiful white marlin.

"Boy, I would love to catch a fish like that," he said. It turned out that he loved fishing as much as I did. "I'll be back in a little while," he told me enthusiastically. I had made a friend.

Randy was one of the best nurses I had during my stay at University Hospital. He caught on to the Alphabet Card quickly and stopped by to chat whenever he had a spare minute or two. That little bit of extra attention meant so much to me. Here I was, without my family and friends, craving human contact, but unable to initiate it or to sustain it very long without another person's genuine interest in taking extra time and effort with me. Randy was a mental lifesaver.

Some of the nurses were becoming familiar with my Alphabet Card, but time constraints limited their use of it to a bare minimum. Others were unfamiliar with the system, so I was back to the guessing-game stage, blinking out yes and no to their tries. And then there were the doctors, X-ray technicians, and the blood and respiratory teams, who knew nothing about my communication card. In fact, some of them couldn't even understand the sign over my bed that explained that one blink meant yes and two meant no.

One night a member of the respiratory team came in and gave me my 10:00 treatment. Thirty minutes later, another team member entered the room.

"Have you had your 10:00 treatment?" she asked. I blinked once. "Let's see now, one blink means no and two means yes."

She promptly began another treatment on my sore lungs. If I could have used my hands, I think I would have strangled her.

Difficulties in communicating with the staff were not my only problems. A nurse brought in a pair of white hose one day. She explained that they were to be worn most of the time to prevent blood clots from forming in my legs. At first they were tight and uncomfortable. In a few hours, my feet felt as if I had walked over red-hot coals. But a blood clot could kill me, so I had to suffer a fire that burned from my knees to my toes for 23 out of every 24 hours—the one-hour break granted to me because I raised cain about the incredible pain. This continued for another three months.

The doctors were also concerned about bedsores, so they ordered me turned every two hours instead of every four. I was moved from my left side, to my back, to my right side repeatedly—around the clock. All this shifting, plus the lung treatments, prevented me from ever getting a good night's rest. But I was told this procedure would be necessary until I became more mobile—a prospect they considered highly unlikely.

I had still been doing my breathing exercises. Convinced that I was bound to have some results soon, I increased the number of breaths to 300 at a time. I would never give up.

On Friday, April 24, Dr. Whitehill decided that I needed more nourishment. The IV was not enough. The next day, I was scheduled for a gastrostomy. An incision would be made and a tube inserted into my stomach. Through this tube, I would receive my food and medication.

The operation went smoothly. As the drugs began to wear off, I felt a dull ache in my stomach. Considering everything else I'd been through, it wasn't too bad.

A clear plastic tube projected from my stomach. This was attached to a machine that pumped a chalky white substance called Ensure into me constantly—my nourishment. Several times a day, the nurses disconnected the pump and used a syringe to force medicine into my stomach. The pressure created from the syringe made my stomach feel like an inflated balloon.

I was still feeling like a creature from outer space. The stomach pump often clogged. This set off a loud beep until a nurse came to fix it. On my right side was the respirator connected to my throat. On the left was the frequently noisy feeding machine connected to my stomach. Above the bed was an IV tube running into each arm, and a tube connected to my nose. It took all my inner strength to deal with this. I had to believe that I would recover, but the reality of my dependence upon so many machines performing so many bodily functions was inescapable.

That weekend I got a new roommate. Pessimistic John, who'd pegged me for a goner, was transferred, and his place was taken by John Howard Marshall. Everyone called him Howard, except me—I called him John. In the months ahead, we became good friends.

John owned a small logging operation near Lynchburg, Virginia. While he was cutting timber, a tree had fallen on him and broken his neck. He had suffered damage to his spinal cord and was paralyzed from the waist down. He had some limited movement in his right shoulder but couldn't use his left shoulder or arm.

John had just built a new house. I wondered how he would be able to continue the mortgage payments and support his family. A once proud breadwinner had been reduced to immobility.

So many tragedies, I thought. So much suffering. Before my accident, I had not really been conscious of this side of humanity. Now I saw how fragile the human body was. But could one event, one mistake, ruin a person's life? Not if I could help it. I heard Kenny Rogers singing, "Every hand's a winner and every hand's a loser," from "The Gambler." And I remembered James Allen, a motivational speaker, saying, "Circumstance does not make a man. It reveals him to himself." I was determined to take the hand I had been dealt and make it a winning one.

Sunday I had a surprise visit from my sister, Pat, and my cousin, Elaine. Pat was such a whiz with the Alphabet Card by then that it was almost like really talking to her. We had a few moments of casual conversation, and then I blinked out a message that shocked her: "Get me out of here!"

"You want to be transferred somewhere else?" she asked. "Why?"

"They killed the man next to me," I blinked out. "It was the respiratory team."

Pat left to check with the nurses. When she returned, she told me that I must have been dreaming. But I hadn't been.

A few nights before, during one of my treatments, the respiratory team had been discussing the case. A patient in another room had been unable to breathe, strangled by a lack of oxygen, and the respiratory team had gotten to him too late. I had said he was in my room just to get their attention. But I was frightened. Several times my trachea tube had become clogged, and it had been almost two hours before anyone came to fix it. I had thought for sure that I would suffocate.

"Get me a private nurse, or get me out of here," I told Pat. I needed someone with me all the time, someone who could summon help for me.

Pat promised me that she would do something in the next few days. Well, I was tired of promises. I was frustrated and scared. I wanted action—now.

I awoke Monday morning, April 27, with severe pains in my chest. Doctors came to examine me, X-rays were taken, and it was discovered that I had once again contracted double pneumonia. The first two times had been like one continuous infection. But for a short while, it had seemed as though my lungs were clearing. Now I would have to be given more antibiotics, and the nurses were given instructions to keep a close watch on me.

I had no doubt that I would survive. The doctors, however, were not as optimistic. They worried about how much additional stress my body could take. Toward the end of the week, another bronchoscopy was performed. This really helped. That weekend I was improved enough to continue my deep-breathing exercises. I had had a week off and didn't want to waste any more time. Somehow I knew that it would not be much longer before all my efforts would be rewarded.

Shannon, the 16-year-old who'd broken his legs, was transferred. He was replaced that same weekend by Tom Bates. Tom had fallen off a roof. Although he had broken both of his arms and wrists, he had not damaged his back, neck, or spinal cord. It would take some time for the breaks to heal, but he would have no lasting damage.

Tom had casts on his arms and hands, but his fingers stuck out so that he could use his remote control box for the TV. He always seemed to be watching three shows at a time. He'd watch one for 10 minutes, then switch to another, and then to a third. It was amusing for a while, but soon it started driving me crazy. The only time I ever got to see one show at a time was when Tom fell asleep. The rest of the time, I didn't pay attention to the television, knowing that just when I got interested in a story, something else would pop up on the screen. Here was another reason for steeling myself for the long process of recovery. It reminded me of how little control I had over my life. I was going to be in control again, even if it took me years! And no one could convince me otherwise.

On Wednesday I had an extensive series of X-rays done. I was put on a stretcher and taken down to the lab. It was an hour before they actually began doing the films. The X-ray table felt like concrete, and I was on it for almost another hour. By the time I got back to my room, I ached all over.

Then an amazing thing happened. I suddenly realized how comfortable my bed was! Until that moment, I was sure that it was the worst bed in the world. But in comparison to the stretcher and the X-ray table, it was heavenly. The bed hadn't changed, but my *perception* of the bed had. From now on, I would try to place all my pain and disappointments in comparison to something worse: I had been dead for a few minutes, and now I was at least alive and stabilized. I saw many other patients who had no hope of walking again because their spinal cords had been severed. Since mine had been crushed rather than severed, I did have feeling and some movement.

That night my spirits were up, and I decided to make another big push toward accomplishing my number one goal: breathing on my own. I did two sets of 300 deep breaths and rested. Nothing happened. Now, Morris, I told myself, in your

whole life, you have never quit in the middle of a challenge—
keep going. I took another 300 breaths and stopped.

It worked! I felt my lungs expand three times. Then I
thought that maybe I'd just imagined it. I took another 300
breaths. Again, my lungs expanded three times on their own!
I hadn't been crazy after all.

Tom and I were watching a Boston versus Philadelphia
basketball play-off. I continued to do 300 breaths at a time, then
a pause. Every time, my lungs did three breaths on their own.
The game wasn't over until late, but I was wide awake. I practiced until the early morning hours, when I finally fell alseep.
When I awoke, I tried once again. Would it really work? It did!
I was still a long way from doing without a respirator, but at
least I'd proved to myself that it really was possible. I didn't
dare tell the doctors. If they told me that it was just a fluke,
nothing really significant, it would have been hard to keep up
my momentum. I wanted to relish the excitement of my first
small victory, which I knew would eventually leave them all
speechless. I'll tell them after I've made some more progress,
I said to myself.

chapter **4**

GETTING AROUND

Action creates motivation.

ZIG ZIGLAR

My head was spinning with visions of all the things I could do once I was free from the respirator. I might be able to start getting around in a wheelchair if I had one less machine attached to me, I thought to myself. Well, it turned out that I would be giving the wheelchair a try before I was able to breathe completely on my own. But first I had another constraining contraption added to my collection.

I will never forget the morning after my first breaths. It was April 30. After the usual cleanup routine and blood work, Dr. Mark Bolander stopped by. He was in training and assisting Dr. Whitehill. Unlike Dr. Whitehill—a bundle of energy, with no time to talk—Dr. Bolander was calm and easygoing. He would always take a few moments to speak with me.

"Morris, we are going to put something on your head to keep your neck straight," he explained. "Your X-rays show that your neck is not lining up as it should, and this concerns us. So we've decided to put a halo vest on you to help it heal properly."

What the devil is a halo vest, I wondered. I sure found out. Far from heavenly, it was a living hell for me.

A man named Richard joined Dr. Bolander. First, a needle was inserted deep into my skull several times on both sides to inject an anesthetic. A metal bar was then placed on each side of my head in a vertical position. Attached to this bar was a flat, thin metal strip that fitted ringlike around my forehead. This was secured to my head by four screws—that were screwed *into* my skull. My forehead was supposed to be numb, but it hurt so much I thought I would faint. Blood ran down my head from the screws, and my skull throbbed until I was certain that it would burst.

Next, a body cast made of heavy plastic was placed around my stomach and chest. Over each shoulder, another mold fit like football shoulder pads and attached to the chest and back.

Finally, the bars on the side of my head were screwed to the body cast and everything was tightened and adjusted. It all fit quite securely. Ah, yes—that's why they had been in the week before taking my upper body measurements!

Dr. Bolander was whistling a happy tune as he finished. How could he be so happy after doing this to me? Now I'm really stuck in this bed, I thought.

The doctor and Richard didn't go far; it was John Marshall's turn next. John had watched the entire procedure but didn't seem too concerned. I guess he didn't realize that I was unable to scream or shout, so I hadn't been able to show any signs of emotion or pain.

Soon John was moaning, then screaming. He even directed a few expletives at Dr. Bolander, but the doctor took it all in stride.

John and I were both happy to see them leave. We'd suffered enough for one day. A nurse came in and gave me a shot, and the next thing I knew, it was 8:00 that night.

My head was still throbbing, but I wanted to get back to my breathing exercises. To my surprise, I found that my lungs would expand 10 times after 300 breaths. I was making progress, but it was still too early to tell the skeptics. Breathing for two days out of 51 wasn't a very reliable track record; I'd have to be patient and wait.

The next day, May 1, I had a new visitor. A fairly young man in a sport coat and tie came into my room.

"I'm Rabbi Sheldon Ezring from the Beth Israel Reform Temple," he said. "Your Aunt Lena was telling a friend of mine about you and asked me to stop by."

After reading the sign over my bed, describing my communication system with blinks, he began asking me questions. In a few minutes, a nurse entered and asked if he would like to try using my Alphabet Card. He was amazing. He picked it up faster than anyone else had, and we talked up a storm.

We discovered that we both loved sports—baseball, football, basketball. He asked me whom I was rooting for in that night's play-off game, and I said I was for Philadelphia.

"I think I'm going to bet on Philly tonight also," he said. I couldn't believe my ears. A gambling rabbi. This was my kind of guy!

Our conversation turned to my accident. He was particularly interested in the experience I'd had while being dead for seven minutes.

"I am tough. I am going to make it," I blinked out.

"You know what?" he said. "I believe you are, also." He sounded truly sincere. During the next two months, he was a frequent visitor. Talking with him was always enjoyable and interesting, and the companionship he unselfishly gave was priceless.

That afternoon a member of the physical therapy department, Carolyn Ford, paid me a visit. She, or another therapist named Maureen Yocum, would come daily to range my arms, legs, and hands in order to keep the joints from becoming stiff. It hurt so badly, I saw stars, but I knew that such therapy was necessary.

Carolyn was affectionately known as "Carolina" because of her Southern accent. She was always smiling and happy. But that day, she was really beaming. Soon Maureen joined her.

"Today we have a surprise for you," she said. "We're going to sit you up in a wheelchair." I was thrilled.

They positioned a wheelchair next to my bed. Then a nurse came in to assist them.

I had been flat on my back for quite a while, so they checked my blood pressure before they started raising me up. When I was at a 45° angle, she stopped and measured it again. She asked how I felt, I blinked once to let her know I was okay, and they raised me to a straight sitting position.

"Are you feeling dizzy?" she asked. I told her I wasn't, and they proceeded to put me into the chair. Maureen held onto the chair, and Carolina came over to lift me by herself. How is she going to do this, I wondered. I'm not a big guy, but she's hardly 100 pounds! It was all a matter of technique. She caught me around the waist, locked her knees with mine, and stood me up. Then she simply turned me around and lowered me into the chair.

I had no sense of balance, so a strap was put around my waist to keep me from falling forward. Next the oxygen tank was hooked up to the back of my chair, and then came the IV bottles. My feeding machine and lung treatment machine were disconnected.

"You can be without these for a few minutes," she said. "Are you ready to go for a ride?"

Before I could blink, we were off. I must have toured the entire floor several times. When we returned to my room 30 minutes later, I felt like a new man. For the first time since my accident, I was no longer chained to my bed. What progress, I marveled.

I had now reached the point where my lungs would expand 20 times after an exercise series. I was still a long way from being free of the respirator, but at least I was going forward. I was practicing my breathing and having a quiet Saturday when a nurse came in.

"I have some good news," she announced. "You have a private nurse coming tonight." That was music to my ears. At 7:30 the nurse showed up, and we spent most of the night getting to know each other. I must have run her ragged once she caught on to my Alphabet Card. I finally had someone to cater to me, and I was taking full advantage of it. She would no sooner sit down than I thought of something else that needed to be done.

When I woke up Sunday morning, she was gone. Will she be back tonight, I wanted to know. The morning nurse said she'd try to find out for me.

That afternoon passed rather slowly. At supper time (for other people, not for me!), I still wasn't sure whether or not I'd have a nurse that evening. I thought about how most of us rush through each day, never taking time to appreciate what we have. I promised myself that when I was back on my feet (quite literally!), I would take time to enjoy the little pleasures life has to offer. Now my days seemed so long that my accident seemed as if it had happened far in the past. Actually, it had only been eight weeks ago. But that seemed an eternity.

"I'll be with you tonight," said a woman as I came out of my meditations. I again went through the process of getting acquainted. She was not the last new nurse I had to break in.

On Monday morning, I had my typical routine. But that afternoon, I had another new experience.

"You ready to go for another ride?" asked Carolina. In no time at all, we were in the hall and headed for the elevators.

Where are we going, I wondered. She knew I'd be curious, and she explained.

"We are going downstairs to the physical therapy department," she told me. Now I was really excited.

I was overwhelmed by the physical therapy room. It looked like a gym filled with all sorts of exercise equipment. I was rolled next to a table mat, and another therapist joined Carolina.

"We're going to put you on the mat," she said. They lifted me out of the chair. While I was lying on the mat, they ranged my arms and legs. Next they sat me up on the edge of the mat.

"Let's see if you can sit up by yourself," said Carolina.

I tried, but every time they turned me loose, I toppled over like Humpty Dumpty. This is going to be tougher than I imagined, I thought to myself.

"Don't be discouraged," said Carolina. "That is perfectly normal after being in bed for so long. We'll try again in the next day or two."

As I was wheeled back to my room, I refused to let myself dwell on my difficulties. Worry and anxiety are energy-draining emotions; I realized that they would ruin my chances to improve. I must take positive action, not sit around feeling hopeless and despondent. M. R. Kopmeyer agrees: "The haves and have-nots can be traced back to the dids and did-nots." Well, I was not going to be a did-not!

Back in my room, I asked myself why so many people fail. I decided that it isn't mindpower they lack, it's willpower. Willpower is the willingness to pay the price for your goal. If it were going to take me days to relearn to sit up by myself, I knew it meant months before I could hope to walk again. The doctors didn't think I could *ever* walk—but I knew that if my will were strong enough, I could make it through the grueling hours of therapy.

I remembered a story told by Kopmeyer that shows how our minds can overrule our bodies when we feel that we must do something. It is a tale of war refugees fleeing a ravished homeland. A small group of men met in one of the villages late one night. They planned on trying to escape to a new life. A woman begged to go with them, to save herself and her infant child. At first they refused. The men believed she would not be able to keep up and would ruin the chances of the others.

Finally, though, they agreed to let the woman and child come. Each of them would take turns carrying the child.

It was hellishly hot, and even the young, able-bodied men were beginning to tire. An old man fell to the ground. "I can't go one step farther," he said. "You must go on without me." The woman walked back to him and placed her child in his arms. "You can't quit now," she told him. "It's your turn to carry my child." Then she turned, never looking back, and rejoined the group. A little while later, she turned to see the old man, child in arms, struggling along.

This old man had overcome his physical exhaustion enough to continue the journey when he convinced himself that he had a responsibility to carry out. My responsibility was to myself, my family, and my friends—as an invalid, I would be frustrated, unable to do all the things that I valued in life, and I would be a drain on everyone, whether they admitted it or not. And there was another responsibility—to others who had suffered injuries like mine. I wanted to give them hope and an example to follow.

The next day, I received a new name. It has stayed with me to this day. As I was waiting to be seen by the ENT doctors, two surgeons stopped by. They began talking about my case and said that they couldn't believe that I'd survived such an injury. One of them referred to me as the "Miracle Man." My nickname was born.

Despite the fact that I did very little actual moving in physical therapy, it was very tiring. The halo vest on my head and chest interfered with everything we did. It was difficult to range my arms fully because my shoulders were bound so tightly. The rubbing of my shoulder blades against the vest was painful. My balance was affected by the weight I carried on my head.

Then I thought of the knights of King Arthur's court. If they could ride horses clothed in heavy armor, I could certainly learn to sit up with that halo on.

On May 5, a Tuesday, I had my usual physical therapy workout in the early afternoon, and was returned to my room. It was 3:00, and I'd barely had time to rest when Carolina entered my room—in an electric wheelchair. Everyone, including the nurses, was interested. It was a rare sight, and everyone was curious about where this strange machine was going and who was going to ride in it.

Wheeling up to my bed, Carolina jumped out. "You ready to go for a ride?" I had no idea what was in store for me but was willing to give anything a try. Once I was in the chair and out in the hall, she put a splint on my right hand to keep my thumb and fingers separated and extended. Then a wooden stick was inserted in my hand and connected to the control lever.

This allowed me to operate the chair BY MYSELF! To go forward, I simply pushed the stick forward. To go backward, I pulled it back. A slight movement to the left or right would get it going in the desired direction.

"You ready to give it a try?" Carolina asked. I blinked out a yes; she turned on the power and walked away.

What an experience! It took an enormous amount of concentration, but I could move my hand forward by hunching my shoulder blades. I could also move my hand sideways enough to control the direction of the chair. But for the life of me, I couldn't pull my wrist backward to make the chair back up or stop.

So I ran into a lot of walls. This was rough on my toes— I was barefooted. But I was like a kid with a new toy. I had gained some mobility and some freedom.

Carolina came back in about an hour. "This chair is going to be yours for a while," she said. "The rehab department lent it to us, and they want it back tomorrow. But you leave that up to me. I'll work everything out."

That night I had a hard time sleeping. The excitement of the new chair was like a shot of adrenalin. And my breathing was progressing. Now, after 300 breaths, my lungs would work for 90 breaths on their own. The pulmonary doctors had noticed a remarkable improvement in my breathing but were at a loss for an explanation. I didn't provide one for them. In the last two months, I'd fought off death and kept in contact with my environment; now my breathing was improving and I could get around by myself. I wasn't about to let anyone pop my bubble.

Thursday, May 7, I took a step toward independence from the respirator. After a morning examination by the pulmonary doctors, one of the doctors told me, "We have decided to turn down your respirator. At first you will feel like you aren't getting enough air. But we think you will be able to tolerate it. If there are any problems, let one of the nurses know, and we will come check on you."

They adjusted the respirator so that it was doing 70 percent of my breathing, leaving 30 percent of the job for my lungs. The doctors didn't understand how this was possible because my diaphragm wasn't functioning. As long as I was going to be able to breathe on my own, I didn't care what muscles worked as long as the job got done.

I was becoming quite comfortable with operating the electric wheelchair now. I'd even managed to figure out how to stop the thing without crashing into solid objects. I did have some scary rides though. Sometimes my arm would go into a spasm, and the chair would run wild. After running down chairs and stretchers, someone would come to untangle me. But at least I could get myself to areas where there were more people. I had been in a confined space for too long, and this little bit of freedom meant so much to me.

That same Thursday, when I rolled back into my room from afternoon therapy, I had another surprise.

"Hi, I'm Nancy," said an attractive woman who was waiting in my room when I arrived. "I came to see if I can help with your communication. I am with the speech therapy department."

Nancy Lumsden stayed for almost an hour and a half. She had no problem with my Alphabet Card, and we talked up a storm. Her pleasant, happy manner was a great boost for me.

The thought of beginning work on another goal was exciting. I was still concentrating my energy on breathing on my own, but once I had achieved that, I wanted to get started right away on being able to speak again. The Alphabet Card was great for now, but it would not do for a lifetime of communication. Just as the electric wheelchair was a stepping-stone to walking on my own but could not substitute for full mobility, the cards were keeping my mind alert and my mental conversational skills in practice but could never take the place of the speaking ability I had once mastered so well.

Friday afternoon, after visiting hours were over and the halls were relatively empty, I got a chance to do some exploring in my new buggy. Carolina came with my chair, got me out into the hall, and said that I should stop by the nurses station when I was finished.

Off I went, turning down the hall to the right—new territory. At the end of the hall, I turned to the left and came face to face with a floor-length mirror. I tried to stop, couldn't, and banked sharply to the left, just missing it.

I knew I had to go back; the mirror drew me like a magnet. With painstaking care, I maneuvered my wheelchair around the hall and headed back to get a look at myself.

This time I managed to stop right in front of it. For the first time since my accident, I had a chance to see myself. The person who stared back was a stranger.

I'd always been a classy dresser, with my hair neatly styled and in place; I actually thought of myself as rather dashing. Now I looked at a person with hair covering his ears down to his shoulders, dirty hair that had not been washed for two months. It was matted and greasy. My sideburns came down to my chin. Instead of a custom-made suit and tie, I wore a plastic vest that resembled a straightjacket. There was no shirt covering my chest.

I was sure that the man underneath was still the same, though. Ten years earlier, at a meeting conducted by the motivational speaker, Bob Proctor, founder of his corporation, XOCES, I'd heard a beautiful poem called "The Man in the Glass."

When you get what you want in your struggle for self
And the world makes you king for a day,
Just go to a mirror and look at yourself
And see what THAT man has to say.
For remember it isn't your father, or mother, or wife
Whose judgment upon you must pass;
The fellow whose verdict counts most in your life
Is the one staring back from the glass.
Some people may call you a straight-shootin' chum
And think you're a wonderful guy,
But the man in the glass says you're only a bum
If you can't look him straight in the eye.
He's the fellow to please—never mind all the rest,
For he's with you clear to the end.
And you've passed your most dangerous, your most difficult test
If that man in the glass is your friend.
You may fool the whole world down the pathway of life

And get pats on your back as you pass.
But your final reward will be heartache and tears
If you've cheated that man in the glass.

Our self-image means so much in life. It is a mental picture that we carry with us, made up of all our past victories and defeats, triumphs and humiliations. And it can determine how we react to a situation—our thoughts, feelings, actions, even our abilities.

But it is not set in concrete; we can change it. It is formed from experiences, so we can change what we experience. Science has proved that the central nervous system is not capable of telling the difference between an actual experience and one that is imagined. If we are unable, because of physical disability, to actually feel the experience, we can create it in our minds.

James Allen once said that, "At any given time a person is where his thoughts have taken him." I could take the path of worry and come to a dead end—a vegetable—or I could take the path of self-confidence and reach my destination—a fully functional human being.

I snapped back into the present. After a few more trips around the hall, I returned to my room and was helped back into bed. The person I'd seen in the mirror was not going to break my stride. With a lot of hard work and determination, my outer shell would once again match my inner image.

On Saturday, Sandy, Pat, and my mother paid me a visit. It was the first time my mother had seen me since I'd left Norfolk. Because of her health, I knew that the five-hour trip had been very tiring for her, but she didn't show it. To me she looked great.

Ashley, Pat's three-year-old daughter, had also come on this visit. As soon as she came into the room, she began to cry. After my recent eyeful at the mirror and imagining how I looked with all of my tubes and machines attached to me, I could understand why. I sure didn't look anything like Uncle Morris. It took her a few minutes to calm down, but she kept her distance for the entire day.

I blinked rapidly to Pat to let her know I had something to say. "Tell nurse to get electric chair," I blinked. She looked puzzled but went to find a nurse. Just as a nurse came in to ask about the chair, Carolina entered. What she was doing there on a Saturday, I don't know, but it sure was terrific. In no time at all, I was hooked up and ready to roll.

In the hallway, Carolina took a few minutes to show Pat and Sandy how the chair worked. If there was any problem, she told them, all they had to do was to cut off the power by flipping a switch on the arm of the chair. Off we went, with Pat tagging behind pushing my oxygen tank.

Halfway down the hall, the air valve on my oxygen tank blew off. It was making a loud hissing sound as if it were going to blow up. Pat let go of the tank and screamed for help. Carolina came running and finally got it fixed. Once the excitement had passed, Pat told me that I was as white as a ghost. All I know is that if it had lasted much longer, I would have had to change my pants.

Sunday was Mother's Day, but the family had left for home after visiting hours on Saturday. It was sad to think about missing the little family get-together we had each year. Next year I'll be there, I promised myself.

I got some good news that day, though. The respiratory team decided to cut my respirator down to 60 percent now. And my treatments would be every six hours, not every four. I was making gains by leaps and bounds.

Ernie Bens wasn't as lucky. Tom Bates had gone home that afternoon—the great channel-switching game was over—and had been replaced by a young boy. Ernie had broken his back by falling from a tree while playing with some friends.

Ernie was also an epileptic. This really complicated his case because every time he had an attack, he would thrash wildly about and have a hard time catching his breath. The doctors feared that during one of his attacks he would break the rods placed in his back and would need another operation. Two weeks later, their fears materialized. And I can't recall anyone ever visiting Ernie. I think his parents were separated and lived pretty far away. I really felt sorry for the poor kid.

The feeling of isolation and loneliness you get when you're stuck for a long time in a hospital bed, far from home, is terrible. It was almost more than I could bear, and I saw family or friends almost every week. My heart went out to Ernie.

I will remember Monday, May 11, as long as I live. I scared two people nearly to death—one was me. I'd had physical therapy in the morning that day, so my afternoon was free. Carolina put me in the electric chair and helped me out into the hall.

"Watch your speed, Richard Petty," she warned as she turned me loose.

I'd become pretty comfortable with the chair by now and had a habit of really opening it up when the halls were clear. That chair sure did move. The nurses got out of the way when they saw me coming. I was traveling at a good clip when I turned the corner.

There in front of me was Delores Dabney, sitting in her wheelchair, minding her own business—and completely helpless. Her neck was broken, and she was paralyzed. When she saw me bearing down on her, all she could do was scream. I couldn't scream. I tried desperately to miss her, but it was too late. With a loud crash, I ran into her full force and knocked her over.

"Oh, please get off my leg," she cried. With all the concentration I could muster, I pulled my hand back enough to reverse the chair. We both breathed a sigh of relief.

Suddenly my hand went into a spasm. I ran over her again. By now, she was so scared she couldn't speak. Her face was white as a sheet, and her eyes were as big as saucers. I'm sure she thought I was a psychopath from the mental ward, intent on killing her.

Finally a nurse came to our rescue. After that day, whenever she heard me coming, she would holler for a nurse to lock her in her room.

Early the next morning, the pulmonary doctors examined me and reduced my respirator again, down to 50 percent. They were amazed at the improvement I'd made in just two days. They left shaking their heads.

After physical therapy, I went for my afternoon spin. I was getting bored after a few routine trips around the hall. I decided to go someplace new.

There was a door leading to a stairwell and a window overlooking the grounds outside at the end of the hall. Feeling bold and daring, I decided to explore this new area and get a glimpse of the real world. I hit the door pretty hard, it opened, and I smacked right into the window ledge; my toes were really taking a beating since I'd become mobile! Contented with the view, I sat there for about 20 minutes. My oxygen began to get low, so I prepared to go back to my room.

With painstaking care, I managed to turn the chair around—no easy task. Then I saw the stairwell to my left. Why I hadn't noticed it earlier, I don't know, but it was making me very nervous. I tried to ease the chair forward to return to the hall.

Suddenly my hand went into a spasm, and, like an amusement park ride, the chair started to spin around and around. Finally, I ran into the rail next to the stairs, missing the steps by inches. The motor was revving up and the wheels were spinning; if my hand moved backward, the chair would go down the steps, and that would be the end of me. Unable to yell for help, I sat there praying that someone would come and find me.

When a nurse rescued me, she good-naturedly said, "I think we better get you back to your room. You've had enough excitement for one day." She got no argument from me.

I was learning that being mobile, in my present condition—unable to call for help, on a limited oxygen supply, unable to fully control my hand movements—was risky business. But then life itself is risky business, and that's what I wanted—to be alive. If I'd made it this far, I wasn't going to start getting too cautious and ruin my chances to really live. Existing just wasn't enough.

That night I reached a major turning point in my recovery, although I wasn't to realize this for a while. The head nurse informed me that a new private nurse would be coming. During the past ten days, I had gone through quite a few. Here we go again, I thought.

It was frustrating to get nurses broken in and then have them quit. There were all sorts of excuses, but the problem boiled down to me. I demanded constant care, and I certainly wasn't a "usual" case. I wasn't looking forward to going through the training process again.

But Ruth Bogard was different. At first glance, she wasn't particularly impressive: sixtyish, short, frail, a nursing cap perched on her head. She worked part-time for Manpower, and I had some doubts about her qualifications. Those doubts were short-lived.

It didn't take Ruth long to establish the fact that she could handle the job. She took charge right away and tried to make me as comfortable as possible. That night, when I closed my eyes to sleep, I hoped that she would last more than two days.

She did. Over the next month and a half, her care and supervision made my recovery smoother and more rapid than it could have been without her. Of course, I didn't know this at the time. She was just another nurse who would probably be gone in the morning, never to return.

Before I drifted off to sleep, I thought about all the gains I'd made so far—more than anyone had expected. I was alive. I was able to communicate by using the Alphabet Card. I was doing 50 percent of my own breathing. I was mobile—not walking, but no longer bedridden. I still had a long way to go, but I was making progress. It was time for a new focus. If I were going to improve at a faster rate, I needed to talk to people about what was happening inside of me. The card took time and required someone who knew how to use it. My new number one goal had to be regaining the ability to speak. I would continue to practice my breathing, go to physical therapy, and improve my control of the electric wheelchair, but my drive, my energy, my determination would now be zeroed in on relearning to talk.

chapter 5

TO SPEAK

Speech is civilization itself. The word, even the most contradictory word, preserves contact—it is silence which isolates.

THOMAS MANN

Each day seemed like the beginning of a new adventure. May 13, a Wednesday, was the day that really pushed me toward my new goal. I'd had a pleasant afternoon. Doug Martin had visited for almost an hour. And he had arrived only a few minutes after Rabbi Ezring had left for lunch. Knowing that so many people were genuinely concerned about me was a more powerful healing drug than any medicine the doctors could prescribe. Those intangibles of love, understanding, and caring were the highlights of my life.

After Doug had left, I'd gone to physical therapy. I could sit up for five seconds without falling over now. I know that it sounds like such a minor thing, but to me it was really a major accomplishment. It meant that maintaining my balance was possible. When I returned to my room from therapy, Nancy, my speech therapist, had a surprise waiting for me.

"I brought something for you to try," she said. The strange-looking machine beside her was a computer. She explained that by programming numbers into the computer, you could form words and sentences. Then you simply pushed a button, and the computer said whatever you had told it to say. A foot-pedal attachment could be used to program the machine, and since I had movement in my right foot, Nancy thought this might work out well.

Out in the hall, sitting in my wheelchair, I was set up near the computer. My foot couldn't reach the pedal, so Nancy got some magazines and placed them under the pedal on the floor. The magazines kept slipping and the pedal kept falling to the floor, but we finally got things somewhat stabilized. Still, it was awkward to use.

There was a book like a dictionary that had thousands of words in it, and the code for each. Every letter, number, and sound had its own code. For example, the word "me" might be number 566, and the word "you" might be 765. Once you programmed the number for the word you wanted, you could begin to construct sentences.

Nancy left, saying she would come back in about 30 minutes. When she returned, she asked if I had learned anything. I blinked once to tell her I had. Smiling, she asked me to show her my progress.

I tapped my foot several times to program a sentence as Nancy watched with excitement.

"Okay, play it back," Nancy said. I activated the playback code.

"Leave me alone," blurted out the machine.

Nancy burst out laughing. "I take it you don't think too much of this computer, do you?" she said.

I blinked once.

"Well, we'll try again tomorrow," she told me, and off she went with her computer.

You can come back all you want, I thought, but I will never accept that computer. I will find a way to talk. Tapping a foot pedal for the rest of my life was completely unacceptable. The machine had shown me how necessary it was to regain normal speaking ability; it had fired up a white-hot intense belief deep within me that I would somehow overcome my physical limitations and continue on the road to full recovery.

Belief in myself and faith in God were keeping me going. Belief, or faith, is the most powerful positive constructive force known to man. Kopmeyer, on one of his tapes, says, "Every religion known to man is based on this power of belief."

The Bible says, "As a man thinketh in his heart [as he intensely believes] so is he" and "All things are possible to him that believeth."

Buddhism teaches that all that we are is the result of what we have thought and intensely believed.

Confucius, the Chinese philosopher, based his teachings on three basic principles: virtue, which frees man from his anxieties; wisdom, which frees him from perplexities; and boldness, which frees him from fear. To attain any of these attributes requires an intense belief.

Contemporary thinkers and speakers have also cited this incredible power that can be harnessed by man. Ralph Waldo Emerson wrote: "No accomplishment, no assistance, no training can compensate for lack of belief." Napoleon Hill states,

"Whatever the mind of man can conceive and believe, it can achieve." Kopmeyer tells us, "Throughout history, man has been told that he becomes what he believes. No problem is too big to solve for the man or woman who attacks it with intense belief."

This doesn't mean a lukewarm belief, a maybe, or an "I think so." There is no room for doubt. You must be willing to burn your bridges behind you; you must go forward to meet the challenge. That's exactly what I planned to do.

On Friday my respirator was cut down again. Now the machine was doing only 30 percent of my breathing. It was exciting to think about how great it would be to have one less machine attached to me. I wouldn't need to drag an oxygen tank around with me on my wheelchair rides anymore, either.

Sandy called that morning to say she'd be up to see me and would be bringing my mother and sister. I was going to have a wonderful Saturday. When I told Ruth that night that I'd be having visitors, she said: "We can't let them see you like this. Somehow I'm going to wash your hair." Boy, that sounded terrific to me! It had been ten weeks since I'd had a shampoo, and my head itched so much I could hardly stand it. But with all that metal hardware on my head, the nurses hadn't figured out a way to get at it. The shortage of nurses and the fact that it would have taken a lot of time to do the washing were also factors, I'm sure.

Ruth got a pan and held it under my head while she scrubbed away. With her fingers, a comb, and Q-tips, she broke up the cradle cap on top of my head. My entire head was covered with sores. Ruth said that she'd never seen anything like it in all her years of nursing.

When she finished, I looked and felt like a new man. From that day on, I never went more than three or four days without having my head washed. Gradually, I was beginning to feel like a member of the human race again.

I was awake early on Saturday morning. I'd been restless all night with the excitement and anticipation of my family's visit. They arrived about noon, although to me it seemed like days had passed. I was eager to show off my electric chair to mother. Two attendants placed me in it, and I took off down the hall to where she was watching my sister's daughter, Ashley.

Mother was really surprised to see me operating the chair by myself. Using her walking cane, she hobbled into the hall to get a better look. In my excitement to demonstrate my marvelous new toy, I followed right behind her. Once again, utter chaos broke loose as my hand went into a spasm.

"Look out, Mother," Pat hollered.

I hadn't seen my mother move that quickly since her stroke. When Pat finally got the chair stopped and turned around, I looked at Mother. She was as white as a ghost. Mother's knees were shaking so badly that I thought she'd topple over. But we all recovered from this scare and had a nice afternoon. All too soon, it was time for them to leave.

Sunday was a quiet day until the doctors told me that they would take me off the respirator for a few minutes to see if I could breathe on my own. I did better than expected, and I was not reconnected for a whole hour. What a milestone! I only wished my family could have been there to share my joy. The sooner I could get off the respirator completely, the sooner I would have more energy to put into my new goal.

On Monday I got the opportunity to work on that new aim. The ENT doctors came in and plugged my trachea tube to see if I could speak.

The procedure is simple. A small rubber ball is placed over the opening in the tracheotomy, preventing air from escaping. This forces the airflow over the vocal cords and out of the mouth to form sound—the normal way we produce noises and words. I tried and tried, but couldn't form any words. I did make some faint sounds, so they instructed the nurses to leave the plug in place for an hour. Then I was to rest for three hours, then be plugged for another hour, around the clock. I kept trying, but with no luck. I refused to get discouraged, though. I was certain that I was going to talk. I could feel it in my bones.

I imagined how it must have been in 1776. Our Founding Fathers knew what it was like to be up against seemingly insurmountable odds. Leaders like Jefferson, Hancock, and Adams were putting their lives on the line; if their struggle was lost, they would surely be used as examples to the other colonists—they'd be hanged or shot as traitors. But their belief was so intense that they forged ahead.

I thought about the Continental Army, formed from a group of farmers who used hunting muskets for weapons. There was no money to pay them, and there were frequent shortages of food and clothing. Yet they faced the well-trained and organized British Army with courage and conviction.

George Washington was a man of such intense belief that his men would follow him anywhere. Without General Washington's drive to attain independence and his troops' unquestioning faith in his wisdom, this brave group of men, hungry and dressed in rags, could not have stayed together through the subfreezing temperatures at Valley Forge.

Thinking about the obstacles our forefathers had to overcome to create this nation helped to put my own difficulties into perspective. I was fighting against the odds, too. The well-trained and organized medical staff didn't believe that I could accomplish my goal—full recovery—just as King George doubted that the uprising in the colonies would amount to much. My hunting musket was the damaged muscles and organs that I had to make function like a fine rifle. My constant pain was the bitter winter I had to survive. Those courageous men and women of the Revolution had made it, and so would I.

When the next set of nurses came on, shortly after the doctor had been in to try the plug, I was asked to blink out the number of hours the plug was supposed to be in. I blinked four times. I wanted to have as much practice time as possible! So the plug was left in for four hours and out for one. It was three days later that the doctor found out about this. He really raised cain, but I'd gotten used to it, so he allowed me to continue this schedule.

Over the next few days, I tried to form words constantly. Even when the plug was open, I mouthed words to get myself used to the mechanics of speaking once more. We take so much for granted. I came to realize that you don't just talk. You have to have your teeth, tongue, and mouth all in the proper position before you can say even the simplest word.

The variety of sounds I could make was increasing, but I'd become frustrated because I couldn't get out anything intelligible. Then I'd remember that if I hadn't achieved my goal of breathing without the respirator, I wouldn't be able to attempt this new goal of speaking. This was because the respirator was attached to my trachea tube, so I couldn't be plugged and use the respirator at the same time. Each smaller goal I accomplished made the next goal possible. I was certain that eventually all of my little gains would add up to one big triumph— a normal life.

Thursday, May 21, Nancy came to work with me. She stayed for two hours, but all I could make were sounds. That night I was able to make a new sound. I tried to form my lips to say something. I must have tried for 30 minutes when suddenly I blurted out "Mama." I really was starting from scratch! I worked hard all night long, and by morning I could also say "No." How wonderful it was to have taken another giant step in my rehabilitation. These were simple words, but they were proof to me that my crushed larynx and vocal cords were working again. If I could say *some* words, I was sure that with lots of determination and effort, I could say *all* words.

Friday morning my head was spinning from all the excitement. I was eager to add to my vocabulary as quickly as possible. The sooner I achieved this goal of speaking, the sooner I could go on to my next one—eating.

Around 10:00 I had physical therapy with Carolina. I could sit up alone for about 15 seconds now. I was progressing very slowly, and I realized that being able to walk again would probably be a long, exhausting process. Taking my goals one at a time made getting from day to day so much easier than trying to deal with all of my problems at once. If I'd allowed myself to dwell on everything I had to do before I could return to life outside the hospital, I'd have been overwhelmed. For now, all of my concentration was going into talking—anything else I accomplished was icing on the cake.

When Carolina took me back to my room after therapy, she said, "I spoke to your doctor today. He gave me the okay to try to feed you some solid food. How does that sound?" Talk about icing!

The lunch trays were being brought in. For so many weeks, I'd blocked out all those wonderful aromas, and now my imagination ran wild. I could practically taste everything I smelled.

Carolina returned with some strawberry ice cream. Then she added some green food coloring to it. "This way we will be able to tell if it goes into your stomach or your lungs," she explained. I opened my mouth wide enough for her to get the spoon in. I tried to swallow. Everything seemed okay, so Carolina fed me another spoonful. But after the fifth taste, I began to gag. Two nurses quickly suctioned my trachea. Sure enough, a green substance came up. Instead of going into my stomach, the ice cream was going into my lungs.

My sweet tooth was ready for food, but my swallowing reflex wasn't—yet. I had two choices. I could see this as one of my darkest moments or just a temporary setback. So far, things that had been impossible one day could be done the next because that's what I truly believed. I wasn't about to ruin a good system now. I told myself that tomorrow would be a new day, a new opportunity for success.

That afternoon I'd dozed off for a couple of hours. When I woke up, a smiling face came into focus.

"I heard that you were able to say two words yesterday. Do you want to try working a little today?" asked Nancy.

I blinked a yes. For the next two hours, we practiced saying vowels, numbers, and certain sounds. Then we would try simple words. First Nancy would show me how to position my lips, teeth, and tongue to form the sound, then I would try to get the air coming out of my mouth to sound like something. At the end of two hours, we were both tired, so we called it quits for the day. I would have the entire weekend to practice; I wasn't going to waste a single minute.

All night long, I stayed awake trying to form words with my lips and speak them. All day Saturday, I did the same. By Saturday night, I was beginning to get some results. Before I slept that night, I'd mastered an entire sentence. I practiced it over and over again. It wasn't very clear, but you could understand what I was saying if you listened closely.

Sunday afternoon, as soon as Ruth arrived, I planned to call Sandy and surprise her. I was ready to show my stuff (or speak it, I should say!) when it was time for her shift. Ruth was speechless. Once the shock wore off, she was as excited as I was.

"Do you want to call Sandy?" she asked, although she already knew the answer. She immediately dialed home and put the phone to my ear. When Sandy answered, I said: "Sandy, I love you."

At first she thought someone was playing a joke on her. Ruth finally had to take the phone and tell her that it really was me. That is one phone call I will never forget. Sandy told me that she was going to call all my friends and family to tell them the good news. When we hung up, I felt as if I was on top of the world.

"It's hard by the yard, but a cinch by the inch," is an old saying, but oh how true it is. I was progressing by the inch; some day it would total many yards.

Monday morning, May 25, my doctors decided to take me off the respirator completely. My lungs were functioning almost entirely on their own by this time so we gave it a try. At first it felt strange. It seemed as if I weren't getting enough air, and it was a struggle to breathe. But by the afternoon, I was beginning to feel more comfortable and more relaxed. About 2:00 P.M. I was taken downstairs to the ENT department, and my trachea tube was removed. The opening in my throat was closed with a couple of tiny metal clamps called staples—these are often used nowadays instead of stitches. My goal of breathing on my own was now complete. This also meant that I could practice my speaking anytime—no more plugging and un-plugging, ever.

At 3:00 Nancy arrived for a speech therapy session. When I saw her, I said: "Nancy, I like you." She almost dropped everything she was carrying. She'd last seen me on Friday, when I could only say two words.

"We'll have you talking in no time," she said. Nancy was so encouraged by my progress that she stayed until 6:00. Before she left, I'd mastered all the vowels, some numbers, and a few sounds.

Those first few words had taken quite a while to come. But now things were moving along at quite a clip. By the end of the week, I was talking up a storm. I had to speak very slowly, and my voice was muted, but I was really talking, and people could understand me. Nancy asked me what I wanted to do with my Alphabet Card. I wanted to tell her to burn it, yet thanks to Pat, it had been such a lifesaver for so long. I told her to file it away. To this day, I hope that I will never have to use it again.

The rest of the week seemed to fly by. Friends came to visit, including Dr. Oden. He was stunned when I actually spoke to him. Soon the shock wore off, and we were happily chatting about a favorite pastime of ours—spot fishing.

"You've got to get well so you can go spot fishing again," Leonard told me. I just smiled. He was probably being jovial for my sake. But I was sure that some day I would be on a boat again, hauling in a huge catch from the Chesapeake Bay. *Miss Sash*, my beautiful boat, was gone, a victim of the accident and my finances. I knew in my heart, though, that there would be another boat in my future, just as surely as I knew that I *had* a future.

I thought about a story Kopmeyer tells in his series, "Kop's Keys." It tells how two black men, John Merrick and Dr. A. M. Moore, founded the North Carolina Mutual Life Insurance Company in 1916. They started with a small, twelve-by-twelve-foot room, four chairs, and an old beat-up desk. Today the company employs over 4,000 salesmen and has assets of nearly one billion dollars. But they almost didn't make it.

Shortly after beginning their operation, they faced their first claim—the huge sum of $40. All they could scrape together was $39.71. The janitor, their only employee, put up the 29¢ so they would not have to file for bankruptcy. The janitor was C. C. Spalding. He was also the bookkeeper and a salesman. With pride and confidence radiating from his face, he showed potential customers how his company had paid a claim in full. C. C. did well. So well that he became president of the company in 1923, a position he kept until his death in 1956.

It would have been easy for Merrick, Moore, and Spalding to give up when faced with their first claim. They might have worried about how they would be able to pay another claim. They might have worried about whether this whole business was worth the effort. But they didn't. They used that claim to their advantage. It proved to potential customers that they really *could* live up to their promises, and that's what sold more policies.

I was going to be positive, too. I had been able to afford a plane, a house, and a boat. Instead of worrying about their loss, or how much it would cost to replace them, I was looking ahead to the future. I was going to recover. And I was going to be successful again.

On Friday afternoon, Sandy called to tell me that she would be coming up on Saturday with Pat, my mother, and my Uncle

Pete. I no sooner got off the phone than in walked Dr. Whitehill with terrific news. They planned on transferring me to The Towers within the next few days.

The Towers is a rehabilitation center that is part of the University of Virginia Hospital. This meant a more intense therapy program, but, more importantly, a return to the mainstream of life. I would no longer be primarily in a hospital setting.

Ruth was on duty when my family arrived, and we all went outside. Life was becoming real again. The protection a hospital offers is wonderful if you need it. I felt that it was time to move on. And finally the doctors agreed with me.

Monday, June 1, was moving day. The nurses came in about 10:00 and started packing up my things—cards and pictures from the wall, clothes, razors, my radio and tape player, all the things that had made a bleak room homey. At 11:00 two men loaded my stuff onto a wooden wheelchair, lifted me into another wheelchair, and off we went. I wondered where my electric chair was. I'd have to ask someone after I got settled in.

Once outside, I was lifted into a van. Five minutes later, we pulled up to the front doors of The Towers—I hadn't realized how close it was. Then we went up to the second floor to my new room. The room had two beds, and one was already occupied—by none other than the pessimist, John Cordle, the man who'd told his wife I'd be dead by morning! I was amused. John was amazed.

After the hectic process of meeting the new doctors, nurses, and administrative personnel, things settled down. John and I began to talk, and we discovered that we both loved to fish and hunt. During the next month, we would have many long conversations about fond memories and future dreams. For now, I was just happy that we could communicate in a friendly manner.

Ruth arrived about 3:00. I wasn't sure she'd be able to work here, and her presence eased my mind. She said she'd checked with administration, and there was no problem.

"Where is my electric chair?" I asked her. She said she'd check on it and be right back. When she returned, I knew something was wrong by the look on her face.

"They won't let you have an electric chair here," she told

me. How was I going to get around, I thought. But those were the rules. I was disappointed, but I'd manage somehow. Perhaps, with the therapy I'd be receiving and lots of hard work, I'd be able to use a regular wheelchair. One way or another, I was going to get around on my own.

On Tuesday morning, the staff wasted no time getting me into my new schedule. At 7:00, a nurse came to get me ready for therapy. She told me that I would have occupational therapy from 9:00 until 11:30, then I'd rest and freshen up in my room, and then at 1:00, I'd go to physical therapy until 4:00. What a full schedule! The thought of being so busy and of having the opportunity to make rapid progress was a real boost to my morale. Who'd have ever thought I'd have come this far in just three months?

At 8:45 I was presented with my new wheelchair. It was nice, but not as elaborate as the electric chair. I felt a bit let down. This was short-lived, however, because off we went to the first floor, where all the therapy rooms were located. I was quite impressed.

The occupational therapy room was about 40 feet by 40 feet. It contained exercise equipment, a mock bathroom and bedroom where they taught people self-care, a raised mat used to teach dressing and transfer techniques—how to get from a wheelchair or walker into a bed and back again. Then I saw a table set up for practicing hand exercises such as writing, typing, and using a telephone. There were almost as many therapists as there were patients, so I was sure that everyone would get the attention that was needed.

I was deep in thought, imagining myself using all of this wonderful equipment, when I was brought back to earth by a voice above me.

"Hi, I'm Lorna Christenson. I'm going to be working with you during your stay here. Are you ready to get started?" Well, I couldn't have been more ready.

She told me that for the next few days, we'd be doing some muscle and sensation testing to find my strengths and weaknesses. For the next two hours, we worked on muscle tests. Then it was time to head back to my room. Therapy was scheduled for Monday through Friday, so I would soon know just how much damage I still had to overcome.

At 1:00 I was taken down to the physical therapy room. It was larger than the occupational therapy room. Along each wall were bench mats. In the middle of the room was a set of parallel bars, where patients were taught to walk. Leg braces, walking canes, and walkers of all descriptions lined the back wall, and there was a set of wooden stairs to practice on.

The atmosphere seemed relaxed and informal. Eight or ten patients were working out, each in a different phase of therapy. I'd been watching everyone for about 30 minutes when a tall, black-haired lady walked over.

"You must be Morris," she said. "I'm Yaffa Liebermann, and I'm going to be your physical therapist." Her accent was unmistakable. I asked her if she was from Israel, and she said she was. I knew we were going to get along well.

For two hours, Yaffa worked with me to see what I was capable of doing. I couldn't propel myself in the wheelchair, pushing the wheels with my hands, but that didn't overly concern her. She saw that I had a fair amount of strength in my right leg, so we improvised. I would kick my right leg forward and grip the floor with my heel, then pull as hard as I could to make the chair move forward.

"Use your left leg, also," she pleaded. But I simply could not get it to work. That didn't matter either. "I expect you to be coming down by yourself next week," Yaffa informed me.

You must be kidding, I thought. It had taken me 10 minutes to go 15 feet. My leg was already tired. By her facial expression, though, I could tell that she meant business. This was going to be more of a challenge than I'd ever expected.

When I got back to my room, I was exhausted. Ruth helped me get back into bed, and I quickly dropped off to sleep. When I woke up at 6:00, I told Ruth all about my busy day and then listened to some tapes until it was time for her to leave. That night after Ruth left, the mellow sound of John Denver filled the room. He was singing, "Hey, it's good to be back home again." For the third time, tears came to my eyes. It seemed as if I'd been away forever, too often out of touch with my family, too many nights in a place I couldn't call my own. My goal of returning home for good was dangling in front of me. More than ever, I wanted to meet the challenge and beat the odds—happiness depended on it.

By the end of the week, I felt more comfortable with my new surroundings. The nursing shortage seemed to be even more severe here than at the hospital. But now I could yell and holler! And that's just what I did, especially when I was in pain and needed to be turned.

In occupational therapy, I'd spent the entire week trying to work my arms. A pole was placed behind my wheelchair, and my arms were put in slings and raised to shoulder level. Then I would try to work my shoulders and arms as much as possible. With effort, I could push my arms downward. When I relaxed, the elastic straps connected to the sling would pull my arms back to shoulder height. The purpose of all this was to get some motion in my shoulders so that I could eventually feed myself this way.

In physical therapy, I'd been working on rolling from side to side and moving from my wheelchair to a mat and back again. The transfer from mat to chair required a thin wooden board placed under me, one end on the edge of my chair and the other placed on the edge of the bed. Then the therapist slid me along the board until I was sitting in the chair.

"In time you will learn to do this all by yourself," Yaffa said. I guess that didn't sound more unlikely than anything else I had done.

The worst part of physical therapy was the 30 minutes a day Yaffa spent trying to open my fingers. It was sheer torture. My hands were balled up into tight fists, and Yaffa was trying to loosen them up. She would take each finger, one at a time, and open them as much as she could. Sometimes I couldn't help hollering, but I soon learned that this made matters worse because the louder I yelled, the harder Yaffa stretched my fingers. I soon caught on and tried to hold my tongue.

The best part of my new surroundings was that I had a phone! Sandy had called the telephone company and arranged for a private phone to be put in my room. She had cleared it with administration, and the only restriction I had was that I could only use it when Ruth was on duty. This was because I could not use my hands, so someone had to hold the receiver next to my ear for me to talk. They just didn't have enough nurses to be tied up for such nonemergency services. It was great being able to talk to my family and friends, to feel as if I really was part of society once again.

The ability to speak was an important stepping-stone on my way to recovery. Now I could communicate my needs sooner and more easily. I had contact with my loved ones. People saw me as less of an invalid, so they treated me differently. It all added up to a huge boost in my morale. I was beginning to see my progress clearly as I looked back at all the goals I'd accomplished so far. Each goal brought me closer to my ultimate aim of complete rehabilitation. Focusing on one goal at a time made me concentrate my energies instead of diluting them by trying to do too many things at once. And every time I completed a supporting goal, I got a good dose of positive feedback. I could say to myself, "Hey, you're really making progress! Keep up the good work!"

"Morris," I told myself, "you've committed yourself to this goal, and there's no turning back. You hard-headed old salesman, you're gonna make it."

chapter **6**

TO EAT

'Tis not the meat, but 'tis the appetite
Makes eating a delight.

SIR JOHN SUCKLING

Making it is one thing; enjoying it is another. Although my unbelievable progress was a miracle, I was still missing out on one of the basic pleasurable experiences of life—eating. The taste of the Mountain Dew I'd had on the trip from Norfolk General to Charlottesville almost two months ago was still vivid on my tongue. Memories of the green-colored strawberry ice cream that I had two weeks ago teased my taste buds over and over again.

I had other goals to focus on, so wishing for gastronomic gratification—food—would only have drained needed energy away from more important aims. I simply blocked out the smells. But I wasn't always successful. Sometimes I caught myself lusting after my neighbor's meat loaf or drooling over his breakfast juice. Mealtimes were constant reminders of my inability to swallow. I recall one time, shortly after moving into the University of Virginia Hospital, when the morning food trays were brought out. How I envied everyone enjoying the bacon, eggs, toast, and juice—and the aromas were driving me crazy! Then the man across from me started complaining about his eggs; they didn't taste good. Shut up, I thought to myself. You don't know how fortunate you are.

Now that my jaw had healed enough to speak, I was anxious to begin eating as well. How much longer would it take before I could swallow again? How many more days, or weeks, or months would I have to endure being fed through a stomach tube? When would I be able to feel the texture and savor the taste of real nourishment again?

Ah, yes, *nourishment*. I thought of Dr. Shears and the perfectly balanced diet I had maintained before the accident. Because I had been in excellent shape—physically and *chemically*— I probably lived through more surgical procedures and bouts of pneumonia than the average person. Now, with the meager sustenance I was receiving through my stomach tube, I could not possibly build up my strength enough for the demands of an intensive rehabilitation program. When I was fed intravenously, I felt that I was being slowly poisoned by all the sugar dripping into my veins. Since April 24—it was now June 6—I'd been living off a substance called Ensure. Everything I'd learned from Dr. Shears told me that no single diet is good for everyone. So how could this standardized stuff meet my unique needs? Because everyone has a different body chemistry, foods that are good for you may not be good for me; what is too much of a particular vitamin for you might not be enough for me.

Well, if the doctors weren't going to take care of my nutritional needs, I was. After all, they hadn't told me to start my breathing exercises. And they had suggested that I practice speaking for only an hour—not the four hours I'd managed to get by taking advantage of the nursing staff's shift change. I'd just have to take care of this myself, too.

On Saturday, June 6, I slept later than usual. The past week had been tiring—a new room, new routines, new challenges in therapy. I didn't have therapy on the weekends, and, of course, I didn't have to be awake for *breakfast*, so it was almost 9:00 before I opened my eyes. By 10:00, I was dressed and resting in bed.

Noticing that my roommate, John Cordle, was awake, I started up a conversation about hunting and fishing. Over the last five days, I'd discovered that good old pessimistic John was actually a pleasant fellow. Our love of the outdoors kept us busy with discussions on various sports and the telling of favorite stories. I had a good one for him but had to save it for another time. His relatives began arriving for a busy day of visiting.

"John's wife, Mozelle, came in about 10:30. She was a wonderfully loyal partner. A friend of theirs had lent her a mobile camper, and every night for the past week, she had been with John from 6:00 until 10:30 or 11:00. And she planned on staying until John was well enough to leave.

Then, around noon, two of John's sons and their families came by. Like their father, they were down-to-earth folks— truly enjoyable company. All the activity and having people to talk to made the day pass quickly. Before I knew it, it was 4:00 and time for Ruth to arrive.

"Would you mind going to get me an orange freeze?" I asked her almost as soon as she stepped in the door.

"An orange what?" she wanted to know.

I explained. There was a Howard Johnson's across the street where they sold all kinds of milk shakes and ice cream. What I wanted was a drink made of orange sherbet and orange juice blended together.

"Do you think you can swallow it?" Ruth asked. I told her I was going to give it a try. She told me she'd be back as soon as possible, and left. I hoped that she wouldn't stop at the nurses station first; they wouldn't allow her to bring me anything.

But I was tired of waiting for someone official to start me back on real food. I would never be able to swallow if I didn't TRY. I was going to bend the rules until they snapped, if that's what it took. Thinking about why people don't succeed, I realized that many times it is because they are afraid to fail—so they don't even TRY. Remember Babe Ruth, I said to myself. He set a major league record of 714 home runs, but he struck out 1,330 times—more than any player in major league history. He had to swing, and swing *hard* to get those homers. And Ty Cobb, look at his record. He was thrown out while trying to steal bases more times than any other player. He had to get off first base before he could steal second. These two famous players weren't afraid to try—and neither was I.

Ruth returned with my orange freeze. She raised me up in bed and began to spoon-feed it to me. Although I concentrated as hard as I could, the first attempts to swallow didn't work; I was striking out. But I kept trying. With the next spoonful, I made it to first base. I could feel the icy sweetness slip along my tongue and roll down my throat—I'd really swallowed on my own! I was so excited, I wanted to tell everyone of my triumph, but I knew that would mean the end of my orange freeze. Ruth kept feeding me, and I kept swallowing, stealing second base while the nurses weren't looking. Thirty minutes later, the entire orange freeze was gone—a home run!

Now that I had finished, I wanted to tell the world. I begged Ruth to tell Dr. Whitehill for me, and she promised that she'd talk to him Monday morning. Just then a nurse came in.

Ruth told her what I'd done, but instead of being mad, the nurse was genuinely happy for me. I had a feeling that Dr. Whitehill's reaction would not be so pleasant.

On Sunday afternoon, when Ruth came on duty, I again asked her to get me an orange freeze. This time when she returned, she brought me something else, a cup of chicken soup. Food at last! Despite some minor difficulty, I was able to swallow both the freeze and the soup. Just wait until tomorrow, I thought to myself. They'll finally disconnect me from this hateful stomach tube and let me eat. That sure was wishful thinking.

Dr. Whitehill had already heard the news when he made his rounds on Monday morning. To say he was mad is an understatement.

"You know you could easily have choked to death," he lectured.

But obviously I hadn't, so he ordered the staff to temporarily disconnect my feeding tube and put me on a soft diet.

"We'll try it for a few days and see how it goes," he said. That sounded great. For now, I would still get my medication through my feeding tube. The nurses simply undid the clamps on the tube and plugged in a syringe filled with my medicine. Yet this was not a once-a-day procedure.

I was on about 20 different drugs. Pills were crushed, mixed with liquid, and then forced through the tube. Some of the medication had to be administered more often than others. And some of it didn't seem to be helping.

The medicine that was supposed to regulate my bowels wasn't doing much good. A severe case of diarrhea was driving me crazy. I would no sooner get to therapy than I would have a bowel movement. It would run down my legs and soak my clothes. Back to my room we'd go to get cleaned up and re-dressed. Often this happened three or four times a day. I can't begin to tell you how embarrassing it was. The nurses never once complained, but it was the most degrading and humiliating set of circumstances I'd ever been in.

Then there were the bowel programs. Every other night, I had to suffer through an awful routine. First, I was given two suppositories. Then, every 15 minutes, for the next 45 minutes, a nurse would insert her finger into my rectum and move it around to stimulate my bowels. Next, paper towels were placed under me, and the excrement was cleaned up. At times, I felt as if I'd regressed to the animal kingdom. My dependency on the nursing staff and the immodesty of the entire process were sometimes harder to bear than all of the physical pain. These blows to my self-image and my autonomy spurred me on, though. I will not live like this for the rest of my life, I said to myself.

Thank God, I had Ruth to do this for me. The casual manner in which she approached it made it easier to bear than with an unfamiliar nurse. Yet, when I finally could go home for a visit or for good, Ruth couldn't be there—I lived too far away. The thought of my wife having to do this made me sick to the core. For now, I would just have to keep practicing my swallowing so that I could improve my diet. I hoped that with a better variety of foods and with the need for less medication, the problem would take care of itself. I was going to attack my eating program with determination, focus on a positive attitude, and be patient.

On Monday afternoon, I had mashed potatoes, soup, and a milk shake for lunch. Things were really moving along. After a grueling session in physical thereapy and a rest period, Ruth brought in my dinner plate. More mashed potatoes, soup, and a milk shake. I hope that this bland meal isn't all they'll ever give me, I mused. Then I saw that there was some finely ground turkey included. I'm not a big fan of turkey, but any kind of meat after three months would be a treat. The turkey was more difficult to swallow, so I couldn't eat all of it. An after-dinner snack of an orange freeze finished off my first day of eating. My mind was filled with visions of wonderfully delicious dishes I would soon be consuming heartily.

That evening Sandy called around 8:30. She hardly ever missed a night. Hearing her voice and talking about the day's ups and downs made me feel closer to home. It seemed like years since I'd been in my own house, living a normal life. Sandy's loyal support and comforting words assured me that living happily ever after was not just a figment of my imagination nor an unrealistic fabrication resulting from positive thinking.

After my phone conversation with Sandy, Ruth helped me into my wheelchair with the help of another nurse, and I rolled across the room to pay John a visit. Naturally, we started talking about hunting and fishing. It seemed like the perfect opportunity to tell him the story I'd had in mind the week before. I said that six months before my accident, I'd killed a bear in Idaho—would he like to hear about it? I had him hooked.

In September 1980, I had traveled to Idaho on a bear hunting expedition. My hunting partner, Woody, and I spent four days hiking the mountain range, taking in the incredible beauty of trees ablaze with fall color along our strenuous route. Once we found a bear, the hunting dogs were supposed to chase him up a tree and keep barking until we got there to shoot him. To "jump" a bear, as it is called, may sound simple, but unfortunately, the bears don't always cooperate.

Sometimes, instead of running up a tree for protection, the bear will turn on the dogs and fight it out. At other times, the bear will just keep running for miles on end. Both circumstances are dangerous for the dogs—they are either injured by the bear or become lost in the woods and can't find their way back home.

It was the fourth day of our outing. We had jumped a bear early in the morning, and the dogs had been running all day. By 2:00 that afternoon, we'd lost them. About 4:00 we climbed to the top of a mountain ridge and heard the barking of the dogs in the distance. Their short, choppy yapping told us that they'd treed the bear.

My partner, exhausted from the day's trip, told me to go on ahead to meet the dogs, and he'd come along shortly. When I reached the dogs, I sat down to wait for Woody. There was the bear, angrily snarling and snapping at the dogs.

"Where is your gun?" I asked Woody when he arrived.

"I left it at the bottom of the mountain," he replied. "It's much easier going without it. I'll pick it up on the way back down."

"You mean to say that I have the only gun?" I asked worriedly.

"Don't worry about it," said Woody. "I'm going to catch and hold the dogs on ropes. Then you crawl under the tree and shoot the bear. If you wound him and the bear jumps you, I'll turn the dogs loose to get him off you."

"The heck with that!" I answered. But my strong desire to shoot the bear got in the way of logic, and I agreed. I assured myself that if the bear hit the ground alive and furious, I could get out of the way.

I crawled under the tree, pushing my way past the briers and thick undergrowth. I positioned myself below the bear, waiting until I had a clear shot at him. I let go a shot and quickly tried to chamber another shell, but the gun jammed. Caught in the briers, unable to move, I watched as the bear fell from the tree and landed right on top of me, piercing the air with a menacing shriek.

"Turn the dogs loose! Turn the dogs loose!" I yelled. But Woody just stood there. I thought for sure I was a goner, but in a few seconds the bear died. If he hadn't been mortally wounded, he would have killed me in an instant.

After it was all over, I asked Woody why he hadn't unleashed the dogs. I told him that I was really desperate there for a minute.

"I wasn't going to get my dogs killed," he answered. Some friend! He finally said that he knew the bear was almost dead. He might have been sure, but I certainly wasn't.

When we got back to the cabin, I needed to change my pants—that's how scared I had been.

By the time I finished the story, John was laughing so hard I thought he'd burst. It had been a great day—eating, talking to Sandy, recounting old times. If I can keep up this pace, I'll be out of here in no time, I thought confidently.

For breakfast Tuesday morning, I ordered a banana and orange juice. The head nurse came in to ask if that was all I planned to eat. I told her that before the accident, that's all I had ever eaten for breakfast, just fruit and juice. I wanted to eat, but too much food in the morning was more than my stomach could take.

In occupational therapy that morning, I spent two hours trying to find some way that I could feed myself. Lorna raised my arms in slings, and with a little effort I was able to reach down to a wooden board placed across my lap. When I relaxed my arms, the sling automatically pulled them back up. If a plate were placed on the board, I'd be able to reach it.

Next, Lorna needed to find a way for me to use a fork and spoon. A Velcro strap was fastened around my hand and wrist. In one end was a slot that held a spoon or fork, so even though I couldn't grip the utensil myself, I would be able to get it from the plate to my mouth. It looked easy. It wasn't.

A mock plastic plate was placed on the board across my

lap. Then Lorna took something resembling Silly Putty and made dough balls, which she placed on the plate.

"Pretend these are scallops," she said. For an hour, I tried to pick them up, using a fork. In that amount of time, I managed to pick up two. As soon as I got them close to my mouth, they fell off the fork. I tried not to get discouraged.

"We'll try again tomorrow," Lorna told me. "You'll get the hang of it. You'll see." I must admit, I was becoming rather frustrated. But she's the therapist, I reminded myself, so she should know.

While waiting for lunch, I met a young man named Mark. Mark was in charge of The Towers' sporting activities, and although we'd exchanged hellos in the hallway, I hadn't had the chance to sit down and talk with him yet.

"I understand you were a great hunter," he said. I told him that yes, I had been, and I really missed it.

"How would you like to go rifle shooting tonight?" he asked.

"Boy, would I!" I exclaimed.

"Okay, I'll pick you up right here at 4:30 this afternoon," he told me.

My mind was on this new adventure all during physical therapy. I was anxious to see how I'd do, considering how out of practice I was—and my handicaps.

At 4:30 sharp, I was waiting in the hall for Mark. He arrived right on time, and off we went, with John Cordle and two other patients. Outside, we were loaded into a van with an electric lift. Although the rifle range was only ten miles away, the trip seemed much longer. I wasn't used to traveling, and the jolts and bumps most people hardly notice sent stabbing pains throughout my body.

Once we got there, we were met by a man who helped unload us and then took us inside. The smell of spent cartridges and gunpowder brought back many memories. Mark got a Marlin bolt-action .22 caliber rifle for me and loaded the clip. Looking at the rifle took me back many years. I'd received the very same gun as my first rifle, at the age of seven. Hunting had been in my blood for so long, it was a real thrill to use a gun again.

Our wheelchairs were positioned in front of a long bench rest, and each of us had a target to shoot at. I couldn't use my hands or arms to hold the gun, so Mark held it for me. A long, thin piece of plastic was attached to my index finger so that I could pull the trigger by snapping my wrist back.

It took quite an effort to lean forward enough to sight down the barrel. I told Mark to move the gun up, down, right, or left until the sight was zeroed in on the bull's-eye. Lining up the sight, I tried to pull back my wrist enough to work the trigger. I couldn't do it. I just didn't have the strength, so Mark had to pull it for me.

The full impact of my plight hit me. Almost more than I could bear, I became sick and dizzy. Still, I *was* participating in something that I dearly loved. It was the first time since my accident that I'd been involved in some outside activity. So my emotions were running rampant—upset by my inability to really fire a rifle, but happy that I was no longer bedridden or stuck in my wheelchair in the hospital.

Out of 28 rounds, I managed to score four bull's-eyes. An excellent marksman before my accident, I had turned in a horrible performance for someone of my caliber. Yet, for a few hours, I had escaped the routine, limiting environment of the hospital. All in all, it was worth it.

Two days later, I had an opportunity to try my hand at another sporting activity—bowling. When Mark asked me if I wanted to go to the bowling alley, I was stunned. How in the world can I bowl, I wondered. Mark told me about a new device for handicapped bowlers that the engineering department had devised. They wanted me to be the first to try it.

"I'm game," I said, and we were off.

At the bowling alley, my wheelchair was placed in front of a lane. Then a wooden table was placed in front of me. My chair was rolled up under the table so that it rested across my lap. Attached to the table was a metal ramp that went to the floor, rounded so that the ball would roll down it. A handle with a crank gave the bowler the ability to adjust the position of the ramp. Because the use of my hands was limited, I improvised, adjusting the ramp by shifting it with my legs. When everything was set, an assistant put the ball in the slot, and I gave it a push.

After a few practice rounds, I got down to business. My first ball of the game was a strike! The excitement was overpowering. By the time I had finished my three-game set, I'd bowled games of 139, 147, and 128. The other four patients hadn't even bowled over 100, and most of the scores ranged from 50 to 75. Mark was quite surprised. He told me that I'd bowled the second highest game ever recorded in their program—and I was the most handicapped of all; most of the others had the use of their hands and arms.

Back at The Towers, my scores were the talk of the entire floor. Ruth was ecstatic. I could hardly wait to call Sandy and tell her all about it. Here I was eating and into sports again, even if only on a limited basis; I was regaining some control over my life.

Later in the week, I found out that this was not such a great thing—from the hospital staff's point of view.

I was off to a rip-roaring start Friday morning. I got into a discussion about vitamins with one of the doctors making rounds. I told him that if I could get off all the pills I was taking and get back on my vitamins, I would make faster progress.

"I don't believe in vitamins," he said. A storm of rage swept over me.

"You might be a great doctor, but you are ignorant when it comes to nutrition," I replied. At this, he stomped out. I knew from my reading on nutrition that most doctors get only one three-credit-hour course in this vital subject during their extensive training. No wonder they're so defensive when approached about this, I thought; they can't dominate and control the conversation with a bunch of technical medical terms that only they understand.

After he had left, I was dressed and wheeled into the dining room for breakfast. Since my swallowing ability had improved, I was now taking my pills orally. A nurse appeared and set a tray of pills in front of me. I got my hand under the tray and threw them all over the floor.

"I'm not going to take any more pills," I said. "The only way you'll get me to take them is to tie my hands behind my back and shove them down my throat."

"Suit yourself," she said and marched out.

Needless to say, this didn't sit well with the nursing staff or the doctors. During the coming week, they tried all kinds of pressure to get me to comply, but I stood my ground. Day by day, I began to feel better. I don't believe that any doctor can adequately predict how that many pills will interact with each other.

So now I was a renegade, bucking the establishment. And others tried to do likewise. This caused lots of problems for the hospital. The staff appealed to me to cooperate so that order could be restored.

"That is your problem, and you'll have to deal with it as best you can," I told them. My main concern had to be my own recovery. I wasn't going to be a model patient for their sakes, at the expense of my health. I was feeling better, and I wanted to keep it up.

In occupational therapy that morning, I was introduced to three new challenges.

"Where's your toothbrush, Morris?" asked Lorna, the minute I rolled into the therapy room.

"Back in my room," I replied. What a puzzling question, I thought.

"I'll be right back," Lorna told me. She returned, toothbrush in hand, and explained to me that we were going to see if I could brush my teeth. We went into the bathroom, designed especially for the handicapped, and Lorna slipped the handle of the brush into a round piece of rubber. This made the toothbrush easier to grip. It took some concentration and effort, but I was able to hold onto the brush.

Then Lorna asked me to try opening the tube of toothpaste. Ten minutes later, I still hadn't gotten the top off.

"Try to screw the top off with your teeth," Lorna suggested. Again, no dice. So she opened the tube and handed it to me.

"Okay, let's see if you can put some toothpaste onto your brush," Lorna said. You'd think that gripping a flimsy plastic tube of toothpaste and squeezing it enough to get a little bit out would be easy. It wasn't. I didn't have the strength in my fingers or hands to make the stuff budge. Well, you just need practice; nothing is impossible, I told myself.

So my first new challenge didn't go very well. For the next hour, I worked on trying to pick up objects with a utensil and bring them to my mouth. With the aid of slings on each arm, I was becoming much better at this. I couldn't feed myself yet, but at least I was making progress.

Sensing that I was getting bored with this task, Lorna unhooked my arms and wheeled me over to a table with a typewriter on it. It was an electric model, and it looked fairly modern. A cuff was strapped to my right hand, and a pencil was placed in the slot at the end of it. Lorna turned on the typewriter and told me to give it a try. With the eraser end of the pencil, I began to peck away. At first it was awkward, but I soon got the hang of it. I was actually having fun. After three tries, I got my name right. I practiced various words for about half an hour.

Then Lorna came over and wheeled me off to a different table. My second challenge had gone really well, so I was anxious to see what else was in store for me. Lorna placed a telephone in front of me—the type with a dial instead of pushbuttons.

"Try to put the end of the pencil into each slot and dial the number," Lorna instructed me. With practice, I could dial the numbers one through seven. But I just didn't have enough strength in my wrist to dial the numbers eight, nine, and zero. This, too, will come in time, I assured myself.

Toothbrushing, typing, telephoning—things that most people take for granted—were now tasks I must struggle to master. I was proud of the progress I was making. Every day I was a little closer to becoming a self-sufficient, independent human being again.

I returned to my room for lunch only to discover more ground turkey. This meat was ruining my appetite. I refused to eat it. Maybe I'd been wrong to get angry with that guy who complained about his eggs; maybe he'd had terrible tasting eggs served to him over and over again; maybe they'd been ruining *his* appetite. At least I had Ruth to go out and get me something else.

As I sat there staring at my plate, someone tapped me on the shoulder. Oh, no, I thought, a lecture from the nursing staff about how I should eat my meals so that I can get better. But it wasn't a nurse; it was my old friend, Landon Browning, who'd been helping out with some of my business dealings.

"Will they let you go outside?" he asked.

"Let's go!" I said excitedly. For an hour, he wheeled me around the grounds, and we talked about old times. It was great to be outside having a conversation with a friend. Then it was over. Landon said he wanted to visit his mother, who lived about an hour's drive away.

Back upstairs, I waited for a member of the physical therapy department to come get me. At least they'd taken away that awful-looking turkey! A man came in, sat down beside me, and started talking. He was wearing a sport coat and tie and didn't look like a doctor. Then he introduced himself as the chaplain for The Towers.

"I've heard about you," he said. "Would you mind if I stopped by one evening and talked with you?" I told him that I would welcome a visit, and we chatted. The subject of heaven and hell came up in our conversation.

"Don't worry about my soul," I told him. "I know, without a doubt, that I'm going to heaven when I die."

"How do you know?" he asked.

"Because I have already been to hell a hundred times," I replied. That left him speechless. Finally he mumbled something to the effect that I most surely had. About that time, someone came to take me downstairs to physical therapy, and the chaplain left, saying he'd be back to see me in the next day or two. I'm sure you will be, I thought to myself. You've probably got quite a few questions on your mind.

I hated weekends. You were supposed to rest and relax on Saturday and Sunday, but all I could think about was the two days of therapy I was missing. If possible, I would have worked seven days a week, and evenings, too! Every time I practiced a skill, exercised a muscle, or learned a new way to perform an old task, I was closer to reaching my goal of full recovery. My main focus was still on improving my swallowing ability—a necessary step toward strengthening my body so that I could achieve better results in therapy. Without proper nutrition, I was not only unable to increase my stamina, I was risking my life.

I had been on a glucose drip—mostly sugar—for 45 days. After that, my only source of sustenance, for 43 days, had been Ensure—a liquid food designed to provide balanced nutrition similar to the average daily diet, containing over 50 percent carbohydrates (mostly hydrolyzed cornstarch and sucrose—sugar). Because I had no fiber or roughage in my diet, it was not surprising that my diarrhea continued. If the hospital staff wasn't going to vary my diet, I was going to start losing ground—

at least there were some added vitamins and minerals in the Ensure. Now I was consuming milk shakes and orange freezes (at least I was getting some protein from the milk and some vitamin C from the juice). No wonder I had had pneumonia three times. No wonder I didn't have the strength to squeeze a tube of toothpaste. The more I thought about it, the more determined I became to get back on a nourishing diet. I was on a collision course with the hospital staff. The crash came on Monday, June 16.

Monday. Lunchtime. More chopped turkey. Again I refused to eat it. Supper was the same. Dr. Bolander came in and instructed the nurses to hook up my stomach tube.

"As soon as you decide to start eating, we will unhook it once again," scolded the doctor. I looked at him with disbelief.

"If you would give me something to eat besides chopped turkey, I *would* eat!" I told him. But he refused to give an inch.

"Just eat what we give you, and then maybe we will start feeding you something different." With that, he left.

I was furious. As soon as he had gone, I took my right hand and worked it under the tube in my stomach. Then I tried as hard as I could to pull it out. I must have worked on it for almost an hour, but it wouldn't budge. I rested for about 20 minutes and went at it again. It took another hour before I finally broke the stitches, and the tube fell on the floor. Blood was running out of my stomach, soaking my clothes, the sheets, and the floor in a river of red. Then a nurse walked in.

"What in the world happened?" she exclaimed.

"I don't know," I replied. "I was just sitting here and the tube fell out." Of course, she knew I was lying. It took some time, but she did manage to stop the bleeding.

The next morning, Dr. Whitehill arrived, madder than that bear in Idaho.

"We're going to have to send you back to surgery and put another tube in your stomach," he informed me.

"You'll have to do it without my consent," I shot back. "I refuse to sign a consent form. Now maybe you'll start feeding me something besides chopped turkey." You could almost see the steam coming from his nostrils as he left the room. We'd had our collision. I felt as if I'd made it through the crash with flying colors, but I'd have to wait and see—I wasn't exactly free to walk out if they didn't improve my meals.

That same day, two occupational therapists paid me a visit.
"We came to help you practice dressing," they told me,
as they got a pair of socks out of my closet.

"Let's see you try to put these on," one of them said.

"You must be kidding!" I replied. She assured me she was
not.

I struggled for about 15 minutes without making any progress. One of the therapists put my socks on for me.

"I'll take a couple pairs of your socks with me when I
leave," she said. "Then I can sew on some large straps with
loops on them. That way, you'll be able to get your hand in
the loop and pull your socks up."

Next on the agenda were my pants. She hooked large loops
through the belt loops on each side of one pair of pants. Holding
on to these loops, I could drop my pants to the floor without
bending, get my feet into them, and then pull them up. It
sounds easy, but it took another 15 minutes before I got them
up to my waist. Fastening them was quite a different matter.
I didn't have the strength in my fingers to fasten or zip them.
But the therapist said that she'd take along two pairs of pants
also, sew on the dressing loops, and attach large rings to the
zipper handles so that they would be easier to grasp.

It's all so difficult, I thought. A two-year-old is thrilled
when he figures out how to put on his jacket. A five-year-old
beams with pride when he is able to tie his own shoes. But
adults? Once in a while, we may be reminded of how complicated dressing can be if we had ever seen an arthritis painkiller
commercial. Most of the time, though, we don't give it a second
thought. Yet I had to concentrate all my energy in order to get
on a pair of pants. Every day I could care for myself a little
more. And I was going to keep it up. Dressing myself, like
eating, was an important step in my recovery. As soon as I
could regain some of these basic abilities, I could concentrate
on my next goal—getting around, not in a wheelchair, but on
my own two feet.

By Wednesday I was being served regular meals. I usually
had a banana and orange juice for breakfast. Lunch was something soft: mashed potatoes, carrots, beans, or other vegetables.
In addition, I got finely ground meat. I still had trouble swallowing meat, so there were times when I couldn't get this down.

Two milk shakes, actually more like ice cream and milk *stirred* together, topped off lunch. Supper was about the same as lunch. I would eat part of it, then send Ruth to the Howard Johnson's to get me an orange freeze and a grilled cheese—I had no problems getting these down. The doctors were keeping strict records of everything I ate. They wanted to be sure I didn't die of malnutrition. I could only wonder why it had taken them this long to become concerned.

So now it was time to move on to my next challenge. Trying to achieve my new goal, walking, was going to make speaking and eating seem like easy successes!

chapter 7

TO WALK

*The journey of 1,000 miles begins with a
single step.*

ANCIENT CHINESE PROVERB

I couldn't claim that I'd taken my first step, but I sure was working on it. For a week now, I'd been practicing supporting my own weight while standing. The standing box, a structure about shoulder-level in height, was specially designed for people regaining their sense of balance and use of their legs enough to stand alone. I was lifted to a standing position by a therapist pulling me on a belt that looped around my waist. At first I could only stand for five minutes before my legs gave out, but every few days I was improving, if only by half a minute or so.

Another new activity was placing plastic pegs into holes in a board. My eye-hand coordination was very poor, and improving it was a necessary step toward increased control of my wheelchair, as well as future control of a walker or cane. Of course, this exercise would also help me handle all of my self-care tasks—brushing my teeth, dressing, and eating. What looked like child's play turned out to be hard work. There were 50 to 70 holes in the board. After struggling for an entire hour, sweat pouring off me from the strain of my efforts, I got one peg in the board—*one*. It took me another *week* before I could manage *five* in the same amount of time.

When I became frustrated with my slow progress, I reminded myself of Dr. Rish's words to my family shortly after the accident and my neck operation: "If he survives, he will be paralyzed, only able to blink his eyes the rest of his life. The most hope I can give you is that in 20 months he might, and I emphasize the word *might*, be able to sit in a wheelchair without being strapped in."

Here it was, the middle of June, just three short months since the accident, and I was propelling myself in my wheelchair, could almost get in and out of it by myself with the help of a sliding board, and could actually *stand up* on my own two feet for five minutes. Putting things in perspective by reviewing the goals I *had* accomplished and the tremendous progress I'd made above and beyond what the doctors had ever expected of me, really boosted my morale.

I often thought of Teddy Roosevelt. Despite being born with a frail, sickly body, asthma, and weak eyes, Roosevelt went from the New York State Assembly to the leadership of the Rough Riders in the Spanish-American War to New York's governorship to the presidency. In his youth, he worked out in the gymnasium his father had built for him at home and exercised his mind by reading books and attending Harvard University. Teddy Roosevelt had not accepted his physical handicaps as unalterable. I wasn't going to, either.

It wasn't a "special something" that made Roosevelt such an outstanding success. It was his ability to tap that inner source of strength and energy that we all have within us. Kopmeyer tells a story about a small, frail woman, just an average person, who was driving across Texas with her son. The right front tire went flat, and they stopped to change it. As her son crawled under the jacked-up car, the jack slipped, and the car fell on his chest.

"I'm dying," gasped the son. In the desert, miles away from anything, no cars in sight, the mother was her boy's only chance of survival. Without any conscious thought, she reached down—all 95 pounds of her—and lifted the car up long enough for her son to crawl out. That car weighed 5,000 pounds.

I wanted to succeed as much as Roosevelt had. I wanted to walk, to have a real life as much as that woman wanted to save the life of her son. As long as I could picture myself walking, could believe that it was possible, and could concentrate all my energy on preparing my body for that first step, it was only a matter of time before I began my journey of 1,000 miles.

Tuesday afternoon, June 17, gave me the encouragement I needed to forge ahead toward my new goal. After my usual ranging and stretching exercises, Yaffa had me get back into my wheelchair.

"Follow me," she said. It sounded as if she had something new for me to try, and she did. We stopped beside the parallel bars. Guiding my wheelchair from behind, Yaffa positioned me between the bars. It was 20 feet to the other end. To me, it looked like a mile.

Yaffa lowered the bars by turning a handle until they were waist level. Then she left for a minute. When she returned, Yaffa had a wide leather belt with her, which she strapped around my waist. Another therapist joined us.

"Okay, stand up," instructed Yaffa. She placed my hands on the bars and told me to push as hard as I could. I tried— *really* tried—but I just couldn't get to my feet. So Yaffa grabbed me from behind by the belt and yanked me up to a standing position. My legs started shaking and wobbling; they felt about as firm as overcooked spaghetti. It took all the concentration and effort within me to keep from falling over.

"Don't worry," assured Yaffa. "I won't let you fall. Now, let's try to take a step forward." So I slid my left foot forward and tried to take a step with my right foot. My knee buckled; here comes the floor, I thought to myself. But Yaffa had a firm grip on me. Recovering my composure, I managed to take three steps forward and three steps back to my chair. Even this minor accomplishment required quite a bit of Yaffa's help. She held me up and had to slide my hands along the bars. But it was a start. I couldn't wait to get back to my room and call Sandy to tell her of my latest success. Then I'd take a rest before supper.

On the way to my room, my plans were changed. I passed Mark in the hall.

"How would you like to go to archery with us?" he asked.

"That would be great," I said. "But how in heaven's name am I going to pull a bow?" Any chance to get out was terrific, but I wanted to participate, not just watch.

"Don't worry about that. We use crossbows," Mark replied.

Fifteen minutes later, Mark, two of his assistants, four other patients, and I headed for the occupational therapy room. On the far wall was an archery target with a net behind it. I had thought we would get into the van and head for an archery range, but this was much better as far as I was concerned. I liked to escape the hospital surroundings, but I didn't particularly relish the van rides necessary to take me someplace else.

After each of us had shot six arrows, Mark asked if we'd like to take another turn. The first round went rather quickly, and none of us had done very well, so we all wanted to try again.

I got to aim the arrow; the rest was done by an assistant.

He had to hold the crossbow for me, aim it according to my instructions, put my finger on the trigger, and help me pull the trigger. Evidently, my eyesight had not been damaged. Despite the lack of control I had over the bow, I got four bull's-eyes out of the next six arrows. Everyone was amazed, including me. I was so excited that I could hardly eat supper that night, and I was also so busy telling Ruth about the day's thrilling events. Then Ruth dialed Sandy, and I told *her* about my exciting day. She couldn't believe that I wasn't stretching the truth, and Ruth finally had to get back on the phone to convince her that I wasn't crazy and that I was making tremendous progress.

I guess such a wonderful natural high couldn't last forever. On Wednesday afternoon, I was on the other side of the emotional scale. David Rodwell, director of the spinal cord rehabilitation program at The Towers, visited me while I was in physical therapy. He told me that I was scheduled to go on a tour of the Woodrow Wilson Rehabilitation Center the next day.

For the last week, I'd been hearing about Woodrow Wilson from other patients. The word was that if you were transferred there, it was like being sent to a concentration camp. One rumor really frightened me: if you were unable to dress yourself in the morning, they just left you there to rot.

Yaffa tried to calm my fears. She took time to tell me about the center, located in Fishersville, about 35 miles away. In 1947 Virginia had converted an Army hospital into the country's first rehabilitation center owned and operated by a state. Since then, twelve more state centers had been established across the United States.

"Just go there tomorrow with an open mind," Yaffa suggested. "I think you will be pleasantly surprised." Her positive attitude helped me quite a bit, but I must admit that I was still apprehensive.

"Now I have some good news for you," she continued. "We called your wife this morning, and she and your sister are coming up this Saturday. We're going to have a progress meeting with them. All of your doctors and therapists will be there. The purpose of the meeting is to bring you and your family up to date on where you are now and where we plan to go with your rehabilitation."

That sounded just fine. I was eager to see Sandy and Pat,

and it was time for me to hear about how others viewed my progress. I expected a lot of negative feedback from the doctors and nurses. The therapists would probably be more positive. But no matter what anyone said, I was determined not to be SNIOP'ed—"susceptible to the negative influence of other people," as Zig Ziglar says—into giving up. I was going to have to really gear myself up for this meeting, get psyched up like an athlete before an important game. If I didn't come out of this meeting with my self-confidence intact, my recovery would be set back for weeks, even months. I wasn't about to let that happen!

Meanwhile, I had the tour of Woodrow Wilson to contend with. At 9:00 Thursday morning, about ten nurses and therapists, and an equal number of patients, assembled in the hallway. Waiting for us outside was a yellow bus with the words "Woodrow Wilson Rehabilitation Center" printed on its side in bold black letters. The bus had an electrically operated ramp to lift our wheelchairs, similar to the ramp on the vans we used for recreational therapy.

In 20 minutes, we were ready to roll. Straps connected to the floor and secured to the bottom of our wheelchairs were there to prevent a spill if we had an accident or had to stop suddenly.

The trip took about 45 minutes, but it seemed like days. Old and badly in need of new shocks and springs, the bus jarred and jolted me, making my neck and shoulders ache. My buttocks and the backs of my legs were burning from the pressure created by sitting in one position for too long. Many patients could get relief by pushing themselves up from the chair, using their hands. But this required a degree of strength in the shoulders that I simply did not have. In the hospital, someone would stand in front of me, lock knees with mine, and catch hold of my pants at the waist in order to stand me up and give me a few minutes of relief. Here in the bus, I had to grin and bear it.

As I gazed out the window, taking in the beauty of the mountains, I couldn't shake the visions of pressure sores I'd seen in a film. Some of these sores required surgery to remove; some never healed properly; some of them looked so horrible that they almost made me sick. These visions of beauty and ugliness mirrored my mixed emotions about Woodrow Wilson.

It could be the next step toward my dream of full recovery—or a horrible nightmare. I'd just have to wait and see.

My first impression of Woodrow Wilson was surprisingly positive. In contrast with the rickety old bus, there stood a modern two-story building. We rode an elevator to the second floor in pairs, then proceeded down the hall to the hospital portion of the complex. After a briefing by the in-charge nurse, we got a tour of one of the rooms.

I was awestruck. The room contained four beds, and mounted above every two there was a large-screen color television. Each occupant had his own closet, and there was a table near the bed with remote control buttons for the television and an intercom connected to the nurses station.

And there were windows! Real windows. They opened and closed. You could look out and see the sky and the trees. Oh, how nice it would be to see the outside world more often, I thought.

Near the door was a sink table with three sinks, built so that a wheelchair could fit under it comfortably. The bathroom, shared by an adjoining room, was huge.

There was not a spot of dirt anywhere. The place was immaculate. The walls were freshly painted with happy colors, and everything in the room was color coordinated. Was I in a hospital room or a luxury hotel?

At the head of each bed was a chart that listed 20 different skills, such as brush teeth, tie shoes, ambulatory, and then listed a grade—full help, some help, or can do. I asked David about this.

"It's a system used to grade you on independent living skills," he explained. "The object is to become independent in as many areas as possible with the ultimate goal of having all the markers on 'can do.' "

This sounded like an excellent tool for focusing on specific recovery goals. I formed a mental picture of a chart with my name on it, with all of the markers on "can do."

Our next stop was physical therapy. So this was where everyone was—the rooms we'd just looked at were empty. The room was enormous, almost 100 feet long, and jammed with patients in all stages of therapy. The Towers physical therapy department was tiny by comparison. To the right of the entrance were two sets of parallel bars, each twice the length of the 20-footer I'd thought was endless just yesterday. The walls were lined with leg braces, walking aides, and crutches. Beyond the parallel bars were about ten benches covered with mats.

To the left were an assortment of tables, pulleys, practice stairs, and bicycles. At the far end of the room were about ten large mats spread on the floor. Here, a group of patients sitting around a therapist were doing exercises, counting aloud in rhythm with the instructor.

Continuing through another door, we entered the occupational therapy department. Once again, I was stunned. Every bit as large as the physical therapy room, this room had exercise machines, a car connected to special devices, where a person could learn to drive, tables for games, equipment for hand dexterity development, and an *apartment* with a model kitchen, a living room, a bedroom, and a bathroom. Everything was built for wheelchair use—low enough for easy access from a sitting position. We were told that before you were discharged, an occupational therapist would visit your home and recommend alterations that would make living easier. Outside ramps, wider doorways, and lower sinks were just a few of the usual recommendations.

By now it was lunchtime, and David led us into another building. The large cafeteria was for staff and patient use. Those who couldn't make it here were fed in a dining hall in the hospital. There were two buffet lines, servicing several hundred people. Those people with little or no use of their hands were assisted by aides. The students (all the patients were called students at Woodrow) ate free, but all others paid.

David told us that the menu was changed daily. My lunch of fish, fresh vegetables, potatoes, a dessert, and iced tea was not spectacular, but it sure beat the food at The Towers.

After lunch, we went to the recreational building. It housed a bowling alley, rifle range, tennis courts, full-sized gym, archery range, putt-putt golf course, pool hall, table tennis tables, library, workshops for ceramics and painting, and one of the most magnificent swimming pools I'd ever laid eyes on. The pool had lots of features for handicapped use, including graded ramps a person could use to go right into the water with a wheelchair.

As if this weren't enough, we now entered the theater and concert hall. The ground level was specially designed to accommodate wheelchairs. The regular seats, made of plush velvet, must have numbered in the hundreds. Dominating the entire room was a huge stage, complete with gorgeous curtains.

Our final stop was the workshop building. Classes were given for skills that would put a handicapped person back into the work force, or at least into the mainstream of society. Computer programming, welding, auto repair, hotel/motel management, sewing, upholstery, woodwork, metalwork, electronics, food preparation, and many other courses were offered to these lucky "students."

"Any comments?" David asked. I spoke up first.

"I think it's great and look forward to coming here," I declared. Most of the group agreed, but several patients were adamantly against the place. They said there was no way they would ever come back.

The trip home started out quietly. Most of us were too exhausted to talk, and several people were already asleep. I was awake. Every bump reminded me of the intense pain coming from my legs and buttocks. As I was thinking about how nice it would be to lie down in bed, we took the Charlottesville exit off the expressway. My wheelchair lunged, then toppled over. I fell flat on my face as I hit the floor with a bang. The staff rushed over to help right me and to see if I had been badly hurt. I had a nasty lump on my forehead and my neck hurt, but nothing seemed to be broken.

"As soon as we get back, we'll send you over to X-ray," said one of the nurses.

"I have been making this trip for eleven years, and this has never happened!" exclaimed the driver.

"Well, if it can happen at all, it will happen to me," I replied. That got a chuckle out of everyone.

Back at the hospital, the X-rays were taken. They showed no damage, though I could have easily broken my neck again. That night I told Ruth about my trip, swearing that they'd never get me on that bus again.

"Why, I'd rather ride a bucking bronco there than go by that bus again," I declared. We both had a hearty laugh. It made no sense to dwell on the tragedy that could have occurred, but I was serious about not riding that bus again.

Friday passed at a snail's pace. I could hardly wait to see my family and have my progress meeting; it was all I could think about. My preoccupation didn't escape Lorna and Yaffa during our therapy sessions. I simply wasn't concentrating. They asked if something was bothering me, and I let them know that, in addition to the anticipation of the next day's events, my head and neck still hurt from my fall in the bus.

When 4:30 came, I was looking forward to a few peaceful hours of sleep before supper. Ruth helped me into bed. I was about to doze off when she announced that I had visitors. Who could it be, I wondered.

"Hey, Morris, how are you feeling?" It was the voice of my old friend, Fred Day. He'd brought along his wife, Elizabeth, and a mutual client of ours, Worth Norman, and his wife. They had traveled for eight hours to see me. That made me feel really special.

Ruth helped me into my wheelchair, and we headed for a small room that served as the dining area. We had entertainment that evening. A young lady who'd come to visit Delores Dabney, the lady I'd run over with my wheelchair, was singing and playing a guitar. Her instrument, a Martin, reminded me of the guitars I'd owned over the last 15 years. It was an evening of memories for all of us. Each of the couples visiting me had lost a daughter, and the young lady's playing brought back poignant reminiscenses to them. Another memory was still to come.

"I have something in the car for you," Worth said. "Wait here, and I'll go get it." When they returned, Worth was holding an envelope. He handed it to Ruth. She opened it, reached inside, and pulled out a handful of pictures. As she held them up for me to see, Ruth gasped in horror.

They were pictures of my airplane after the crash—or what was left of it. I couldn't believe my eyes. How in the world could anyone have lived through that, I wondered.

"How did you manage to get these?" I asked Worth.

"I took them myself," he answered. He told me that he'd been in Virginia Beach on March 10 for a convention. He'd planned on surprising me with a visit but couldn't reach me; he'd tried all day and all night. It was not until he watched the late news that night that he learned about my accident. The next day, he drove out to the Eastern Shore and took the pictures.

"These are for you," he said. "That is, if you want them."

"I sure do! Thanks," I replied. These photos would remind me that I was lucky to be alive at all. And they made the goals I'd accomplished so far seem like miracles.

It was almost 7:00 when Fred told me they had to get going. They planned to drive back that night, meaning that they wouldn't get home until the next morning.

"Your visit has meant so much to me," I told them. Before they left, we all bowed our heads, and Fred said a prayer for me. Then they were gone. I felt the now familiar mixture of joy and sadness—the joy of knowing friends who really care about you, and the sadness of parting.

On Saturday morning at 6:00 A.M., I was wide awake. This was the big day. Sandy and Pat would be here in four hours, and then we'd have our powwow with the hospital staff. At 7:00 a nurse came in to help me dress and get ready for breakfast. By 10:00 I was dressed, fed, and waiting. Right on time, Sandy and Pat appeared in the doorway of my room.

As we wheeled into the hall, I heard the booming voice of my Uncle Pete. It was unmistakable.

"How do you feel, son?" he asked. I barely had time to tell him I was doing okay before Yaffa came and told us to follow her. It was time for the meeting.

The first person to speak was Dr. Bolander. He explained the extent of my injuries and showed X-rays of my neck at the time of the accident and now. My bones were not knitting as well as they should. There was a good chance that another operation would be required.

Then he compared the spinal cord to a series of telephone lines. He explained that messages were transmitted from the brain to various parts of the body and back to the brain via these lines. Once cut, there was a short circuit, and the messages were interrupted. Without sensory or motor feedback, parts of the body affected by the damage could not function. Because nerves in the spinal column would not regenerate like other parts of the body, the disconnection was permanent. But I felt I still had room to hope.

"One day soon, I will go to Africa and shoot an elephant," I said when he had finished. "I'll show you." Everyone laughed but Dr. Bolander. He just looked at me as if I were crazy.

Next, Yaffa and Lorna explained what we were doing in

therapy, and what their plans were for the remainder of my stay.

After they had finished, Nancy talked about the amazing progress I'd made in speech therapy. She was the bright spot of the entire meeting—so positive and optimistic.

It was nice to hear something good before the nursing staff and the administration gave their reports. Their comments were fairly negative, as they covered the problems that still remained in the areas of self-care and cooperation (or rather the lack of it).

Finally, it was over. I headed for my room, and Sandy, Pat, and Uncle Pete went to Howard Johnson's to get me a grilled cheese and an orange freeze. They stayed for lunch, but then they had to head home. They were returning to their regular lives, and I had to remain to face another inactive weekend—alone.

Settling in for an afternoon of solitude, I thought about how most of us use very little of our brain potential. We simply don't utilize all of that fancy equipment we carry around in our heads. Some estimates are in the 2 percent bracket; I tend to think that we use only 1/100th of 1 percent on a regular basis.

That's such a waste. I once read an article written by a research scientist at IBM. He suggested that if a person's brain could be reproduced in computer form, it would be larger than the Empire State Building. Yet this man-made duplicate could not produce a single thought or idea, something each of us does in the flash of an eye.

I felt as though I were drawing on some of this potential brain power as I achieved goals that the professionals thought were impossible. I decided to make a conscious effort to continue increasing my concentration level. If I couldn't work out in therapy over the weekends, I would imagine myself working out. If I didn't have visitors, I would remember past visits, important events in my life, or imagine what my next visit with family and friends would be like. Thinking about what I *couldn't* do was draining—emotionally and spiritually. Instead, I would concentrate on what I *could* do, as well as what I *would* do, someday.

June 22, another Monday morning, was the beginning of another week. After dressing and having breakfast, I was waiting in the hall to go to occupational therapy when the head nurse started pushing my wheelchair back to my room.

"What's the problem?" I wanted to know.

"You won't be going to therapy. You're scheduled to go to the University Hospital for some psychological tests," the nurse explained. Because I had been dead for seven minutes and had suffered damage to my brain stem, the doctors were concerned about the possibility of brain damage.

About 9:30, my transportation came. The tests took all morning. I was taken back to The Towers for lunch. By 1:00, I was all set to go to physical therapy. Again the nurse appeared.

"They want you back for more tests," she said. Back at the hospital, a different psychiatrist prepared to test me.

He reached into his pocket and took out some change. Laying a dime and a penny on the table, he asked me how much it was.

"Twenty-eight cents," I answered. He added a nickel and again asked me for the sum.

"Why, that's easy," I replied. "It's a dollar three eighty."

"What did you say?" he asked. I repeated my answer.

Next he took a wooden box, placed it in front of me, and put a pencil in it.

"What did I just do?" he asked.

"You put that box inside the pencil," I told him.

"You just wait right here," he said. Then we walked out of the room. When he returned, there were two other doctors with him. They were speaking in muted tones, but I heard the psychiatrist who'd just tested me saying, "I don't know how to classify him. I don't know if he's paranoid, neurotic, schizophrenic, or what." The two other doctors walked over to me. One of them took the dime and penny and put them in front of me.

"How much is that?" he asked.

"Eleven cents," I said. He added a nickel.

"Now how much is there?" he wanted to know.

"Sixteen cents," I replied. Adding a quarter, he again asked me for the total.

Forty-one cents," I told him without hesitation. At this point, the psychiatrist who'd tested me was getting red in the face. The other doctor took the wooden box and dropped the pencil into it. Before he could ask me what he'd done, I spoke up.

"You just put that pencil in that box," I said. That was all the psychiatrist could stand.

"Why didn't you do that for me a few minutes ago?" he asked angrily.

"Because I am sick and tired of taking your crazy tests," I replied. "And I am not coming back for any more," I added firmly. I guess I satisfied them that I still had all my marbles; there were no more psychological tests after that!

That afternoon, after returning from this frustrating experience, I received a call from an old friend, Dr. Tom Voshell. He told me he was going to leave home at 5:00 tomorrow morning with his son, Rusty, and should arrive for a visit about 10:00.

Tuesday morning, I was waiting for them in the lobby.

"Follow me," I said, and headed for occupational therapy. The anxiety of showing them what I could do was overwhelming. I wanted them to see how hard I'd been working. With the heels of my feet, I pulled my wheelchair forward, and they followed behind.

After introducing Tom and Rusty to everyone, the three of us went with Lorna to the bathroom.

"Now, show them how you can brush your teeth," she said. I tried to open the toothpaste, but it was no use. Lorna put some toothpaste on my brush. Despite my enormous efforts, I could only manage a feeble, sloppy attempt to clean my teeth.

We went on to the other skills I was trying to master: typing, dialing the telephone, writing, and eating. I was proud of my attempts, although I knew that I had a long way to go, but Tom was not so impressed. Oh, he didn't tell me that during his visit, but months later, he let me know on his way home he'd told his son about his thoughts. In his professional opinion as a doctor, he was sure that I would never use my hands again.

Tom didn't let me see his doubts that day. We had a pleasant visit, and it was lunchtime before they left. Perhaps Tom didn't want to interfere with my therapy program or with the opinions of other doctors. Perhaps he was just being a supportive friend. Whatever his reasons were, I'm glad that he kept his true feelings to himself. As Muriel James and Dorothy Jongeward say in their marvelous book entitled *Born To Win:* "Man was born to win, but over a period of years, he has been conditioned to lose." Other people tell us we *can't* do things, we tell ourselves that we *can't* do things, and it becomes a self-fulfilling prophecy—we really *can't*.

I believed in myself, but because the nurses and doctors didn't share that belief, I needed my friends and family to help me sustain my optimism. Tom really helped me that day. After his visit, I had no doubts and worries struggling to take away my energy. Instead, I was rested, happy in knowing that my friends cared about me; then I met my next challenge that afternoon in physical therapy.

Shortly after my arrival in the therapy room, I was outfitted with a walker. We tried several different makes and models until we found one that was comfortable. With Yaffa holding onto my belt to give me balance, I began walking. Another surge of pride over my increasing independence rushed through me. All of the standing practice to strengthen my legs was paying off—I could stand at the parallel bars, alone, for 10 minutes now. By the time I left therapy that afternoon, I was strutting my stuff.

The rest of the week was rather routine—breakfast, occupational therapy, lunch, physical therapy, dinner, and rest—until Friday. That day was anything *but* routine. If all went well, it would mean a weekend pass home. Pat and Sandy arrived on Friday for family training. They would have to learn about all phases of my care and physical abilities before I could leave the well-tended environment of The Towers. The training session took all day.

First, Pat and Sandy went to occupational therapy, where Lorna showed them how to use my transfer board to help get me in and out of the car and bed. Next, Lorna showed them how to help dress and feed me.

After lunch, a nurse took over. She showed Pat and Sandy how to bathe me, assemble and connect my leg bag, do my bowel program, turn me every two hours to prevent pressure sores, and other physical care procedures.

Then it was Yaffa's turn. She went over transfer techniques for getting me in and out of my wheelchair and pushing my chair up and down stairs and over curbs. Everything is going smoothly, I thought to myself, but how will they do getting the weight of me and my chair up and down steps? I soon found out.

After Yaffa gave a demonstration, Pat gave it a try. No

problem. Then it was Sandy's turn. Again, no problem. Pat asked to try again. I began to get jittery, but Pat did just fine. Then Yaffa wanted Sandy to practice once more. Sandy tried to decline, saying her back was hurting, but Yaffa would have none of that. Turning my wheelchair backward, Sandy began backing up the stairs and pulling me along with her one step at a time. She made it almost to the top.

Then she lost control and dropped me. My heart was racing as I started to fall. Yaffa jumped in front of my chair and caught me. When she got me back to the top of the stairs, Yaffa again turned me over to Sandy.

"Okay, take him down," she said.

"Wait a minute," I protested. "Enough is enough." But Yaffa couldn't let Sandy leave feeling that she couldn't handle me. Yaffa was a believer in the old saying "The best medicine for falling off of a horse is to get right back on." I closed my eyes and prayed the whole way down. Everyone was relieved when Sandy and I made it to the bottom without further incident.

When Pat and Sandy left that afternoon, I felt pretty comfortable with the way they handled me. They'd passed the training test, and I looked forward to a trip home. It came much sooner than expected.

That Monday, June 29, David Rodwell, the fellow who'd given us the tour of Woodrow Wilson, visited me.

"Everything is all set for you to check into Woodrow Wilson on Monday, July 6. We've also approved a pass for you to go home this weekend. You can check back in on Sunday or have your family take you directly to Woodrow on Monday."

All of this was music to my ears. I'd been thinking about Woodrow Wilson for a week now, knowing that I was going, but not having a target date. Now I had one. The home pass was a real surprise.

David said he'd get in touch with Sandy to set things up. I couldn't wait to tell her about it myself. It seemed like therapy would never end that day. My head was spinning, thinking about these new adventures, and it showed. Both Lorna and Yaffa commented on how preoccupied I was.

The minute I got back to my room, I called Sandy. I just couldn't wait until after supper. David had already phoned her, and she was starting to make plans for my trip home. Sandy was concerned about problems that might arise during my stay and wanted to hire a nurse to help her. Details, details, I said to myself. Nothing can stem the tide now! I was going home if she had to hire the entire staff of Norfolk General Hospital!

Sandy and I talked again on Wednesday night. She had spoken with Pat, and they were planning on coming up together Friday morning. Sandy had rented a station wagon so they could carry my wheelchair, walker, and all the things from my room. And she had contacted someone to stay with us for the weekend to help out with my care.

"He's a physical therapy student at Old Dominion University," she told me. "Also, Pat said she would be glad to stay and help out. We'll be there Friday around noon. Try to get Ruth to help you pack Thursday night so you'll be all ready to go."

My adrenalin was really flowing now. I had to force myself to eat supper Wednesday night and slept very little. It seemed as though Thursday night would never come. As Ruth packed my things, I watched my homey room full of pictures and cards return to its cold, impersonal state. Suddenly everything looked so barren.

Moving can mean the beginning of new adventures, but it can also mean leaving old friends behind. At 11:00 it was time for Ruth to go. She hugged me and told me she would stay in touch. We had become very fond of each other, and it was sad to have to end our relationship.

"I'm really going to miss you," I told her. When she finally left, there were tears in our eyes.

When the nurse came in to wake me at 7:30 Friday morning, I was already wide awake, despite an almost sleepless night. My mental alarm clock had gone off with its usual accuracy, and I was impatient to get on with the preparations for my trip.

The nurses boxed up all the medical supplies I would need, and I got dressed and had breakfast. By the time Sandy and Pat arrived, I was like a race horse at the starting gate, chomping at the bit and raring to go. It took about 30 minutes to pack up the car. Then I bade everyone farewell.

Home again for the first time in four months, I thought excitedly. The six-hour trip would be very hard on me, but the final reward would be worth every ache and pain. As I watched the landscape gradually change from mountains to hills to the flat country that I called home, my anticipation grew. As we passed the Chesapeake Bay, my senses were filled with the old familiar smell of salt air. The mountains of Charlottesville were beautiful, quiet, and peaceful, yet incomparable to my first love—the seashore.

A half hour later, we pulled up in front of my mother's house. After a brief visit, filled with hugs and smiles, we were off for the last leg of our journey. Tears came to my eyes as we pulled into my driveway. Thank God, the doctors had been wrong. Just a few months ago, they'd all told me that I would never see home again. I wanted to get down on my hands and knees and kiss the ground.

Earlier in the week, Sandy had had a ramp built to make it easier for us to get my wheelchair up the front steps. It was great. In a few minutes, I was inside the house—home at last, even if it was only going to be for a few days. Once I was settled in bed for a much needed rest, I asked Sandy to let my dog, Frisky, out of the kitchen. He'd been having a fit, barking and howling and doing his best to break down the door, since I'd entered the house. Depite my four-month absence, he hadn't forgotten me.

The moment Sandy opened the door, Frisky made a bee-line for the bedroom. We had never permitted him to get on the bed, but this time ten dogcatchers couldn't have stopped him. Even though I couldn't reach out and pet him, he didn't seem to mind. He was all over me, wiggling and licking my face.

While all of this was going on, Sandy told me that for several weeks after my accident, Frisky had moped around the house as if he'd lost his best friend. He refused to eat and would go upstairs into my office and sit under my desk all day long. About 4:30 in the afternoon, he would come back downstairs and sit at the back door waiting for me to come home from work. By some sixth sense, he knew that something was wrong.

Now the phone began to ring. Sandy had to unplug the phone in the bedroom so that I could get a little rest. Until 11:00 that night when Sandy finally disconnected it, the phone rang almost constantly. Family, friends, and business clients all wanted to come by for a visit. Tomorrow was sure going to be a busy day.

It was about 8:00 that evening when Craig Brown, the physical therapy student, arrived. He helped Sandy get me ready for a good night's sleep. I was bushed, and I needed to rest for the next day's excitement.

Saturday, from 11:00 in the morning to 5:00 that afternoon, there was a constant stream of people going in and out of the house. It was comforting to know that so many folks cared about me. I realized how dependent we are on family and friends for emotional and spiritual support. None of us goes through life alone.

After everyone had left, Sandy prepared a fabulous meal of roast chicken, mashed potatoes, string beans, steamed shrimp, and homemade cheesecake. It had been so long since I'd had a really good meal that my taste buds were going wild. I thought about how hard it would have been if I had to watch as others ate this delicious food—only a month ago, I couldn't have had any of it. Content and full, I must have looked like the Cheshire cat.

I napped after dinner until Craig arrived at 8:00. He'd left early that morning because Sandy hadn't felt that she needed him during the day. Pat planned to stay the night also and was already there when Craig came.

"Let's go see the fireworks," Sandy suggested. It sounded like a great idea to me. The day had been so jam-packed with visitors that I'd forgotten it was the Fourth of July. We all crammed into Pat's car, a Honda, and took off.

Once there, Craig helped me out of the car and into my wheelchair so I could smell the fresh air and watch the dazzling display of colored lights in the sky.

It was 11:00 that night before we got home and midnight before I finally got to bed. Sunday would be just as busy as today, and I needed my rest, but I wouldn't have traded in a single moment. It had been the most enjoyable day I'd had since the crash. I felt alive again. Now that I knew for sure that living at home was feasible, I was more determined than ever to finish the rehabilitation process and come home for good.

Sunday was over much too quickly. Again, there was a house full of people, radiating a comforting warmth that I would recall during the coming long days of recovery. We all planned to retire early that night, but it was late evening before I finally closed my eyes. In order to get to Woodrow Wilson by the 2:30 check-in time, we would have to be on the road by 8:30.

The alarm went off at 5:00 Monday morning. Staying right on schedule, we dressed, ate, packed the car, stopped for a quick visit at my mother's place, and headed for my new residence. We had sandwiches and drinks with us so we wouldn't have to stop for lunch.

At 2:15 we pulled up in front of the administration building of Woodrow Wilson. I must admit to a little queasiness. New beginnings are difficult. But I was sure that in time I would make new friends and adjust.

After completing some necessary paperwork, we went upstairs to see my room. It was just as nice as the one I'd seen on the tour. Little by little, the room took on a comfortable, familiar look as Sandy and Pat put up pictures and cards and filled the closet with my things.

Once the unpacking was done, a nurse came in and asked us to follow her. She led us down the hall to a conference room. Inside, there were about ten people sitting around a table, each representing a different department of the rehabilitation center.

At the head of the table sat Dr. Thomas Spicuzza, the doctor who'd be in charge of my case. After everyone else had given an assessment and objectives regarding my case, Dr. Spicuzza looked straight at me.

"What are your goals?" he asked.

"I plan on walking out of here on my own two feet, without any mechanical aid," I replied. "My ultimate goal is complete recovery."

"You have to be realistic," he said, looking at me with an expression that told me he'd heard that tune before. "You will never be able to function anywhere close to the level you once did."

"You look here, you darn fool! I'll show you!" I shot back.

The meeting came to an abrupt end.

Duane Anderson, my new counselor, walked out of the room with us. For 30 minutes, he took us on a tour so that Sandy and Pat would have a good mental image of my surroundings. By the time we had finished, it was late afternoon, and Pat was eager to get on the road. Tears streamed down my face as I sat in the doorway and watched them leave. Insufficient rest over the last few days, the long trip, a new environment, and the departure of my family left me physically and mentally drained.

I was startled out of my musings by Betty, the charge nurse, who'd come to check on me.

"Do you have any questions you need to ask me?" she wanted to know.

"I've heard some bad things about Woodrow," I told her.

"Like what?" she asked.

"I've heard that they will let you rot here. If you can't get up and dress yourself, they will leave you for several hours," I confided.

"Who did you hear such things from?" Betty inquired.

"Several of the patients at The Towers," I replied. But then I smiled and added, "I don't really believe it."

Betty smiled back. "We will try not to let you rot while you're here." Then she left.

As I lay in bed, reviewing all that had happened that day, my thoughts finally settled on my afternoon meeting with the staff. I knew that everyone thought I had unrealistic goals, but they would never sell that idea to me. I believe that your expectations can govern your life, so I had no intention of lowering mine because of "professional opinions." All too often, we focus on our illness. We concentrate on what is wrong and fail to see what is right.

It's not really the individual's fault. Society conditions us to think this way. Television commercials bombard us with products for colds, upset stomachs, arthritis, headaches, and a hundred other complaints. We constantly ask ourselves whether we're sick enough to go to the doctor's office. Do we need product A, which will relieve 6 symptoms, or product B, which will relieve 12? Should we take aspirin or acetaminophen—or both? We begin to lose sight of how well we are by concentrating on the sickness. So it is not surprising that when we *are* struck by a major illness, we can't suddenly reverse this trend. Our response is firmly ingrained by years of negative input.

But it's not impossible. A tremendous amount of thinking and persistence and determination to stop more incoming negatives can turn the tide. Many people fail. They get discouraged too easily. What they don't realize is that when they give up, everything goes back to zero, and they have to start all over again. Rolling the boulder only halfway up the hill won't do— you may end up farther back than when you started. This was not going to happen to me. My boulder was going to make it to the top or I would die trying, but I was *never* going to give up.

Blood tests, urine tests, physical exams, medical forms—a ton of information went into my file on Tuesday. Are they just keeping records, or are they writing a book about me, I wondered. Everything came to an abrupt halt at 4:00. Ah, rest time, I thought. But I was wrong. An attendant walked in and helped me into my wheelchair.

"Follow me, and I'll show you where the dining hall is," he said. "Dinner is served at 4:30." With that brief announcement, we were off.

This was an unanticipated wrinkle. I'd been used to eating much later, so it was going to take me some time to adjust. Oh, well, I've coped with more traumatic things than this, I told myself.

The dining hall was for hospital students only. Once you were able to stay in the dormitories, you were expected to take your lunch in the cafeteria with the staff. I will be more than willing to make the trip to the cafeteria, I said to myself as I looked around the room. The sight was bone-chilling. Stroke victims, amputees, people with brain damage, cerebral palsy victims, blind people, spinal cord injury patients, and those with other disabilities I couldn't even begin to describe painted a picture of human suffering more vivid than I had ever seen. Most people were confined to wheelchairs and needed an attendant to feed them. How did I go through so many years of life without ever realizing that these people exist, I asked myself. Because I'd been there, I could empathize with these people who had to depend on others for the necessities of life. I still needed help with my food, but through hard work, I'd managed to become about 50 percent independent. The dining hall scene I encountered that day spurred me on to greater efforts toward complete independence.

After I had finished eating, I returned to my room, and a nurse helped me into bed. She helped me to undress, and I asked her to switch on the television.

"Any particular channel?" she asked. I told her that it really didn't matter, I'd probably fall asleep soon anyway.

"I'll be back to check on you later," she told me. "You get a good night's rest. Tomorrow is going to be a tiring day for you. Someone will be in about 6:30 to get you dressed and take you to therapy by 9:00."

The next thing I knew, someone was shaking me to wake up.

By 8:00, I was dressed, shaved, and ready for breakfast, which was served in my room. As soon as I had finished, it was time for therapy. My new daily schedule would be like this: occupational therapy 9:00–10:00; physical therapy 10:00–11:30; lunch, occupational therapy 1:00–2:30; physical therapy 2:30–4:30; then dinner and rest. It sounded very demanding, but that's what I wanted. I had no illusions about this process of rehabilitation being easy. The harder I worked, the sooner I'd go home for good.

A young lady greeted me as I entered occupational therapy.

"Hi, I'm Julie Westerhaus," she said. "I'm going to be working with you."

Julie was a student doing her last affiliation before graduating from college as an occupational therapist, a practice similar to student teaching in education or an internship in another field of study.

"We're going to spend the next few days doing muscle tests and sensation tests," she informed me.

"But I just got through doing all those at The Towers," I told her.

"I know! I have all your reports," she replied. "But I want to do my own tests because every therapist grades differently. Then I'll know what kind of program is best for you. I'll be better able to monitor your progress also." For an hour, we did muscle tests.

Then it was time to go to physical therapy. There I met Dave, my instructor for physical therapy. I'd met Dave at orientation on my first day, so at least *he* wasn't a stranger.

"I've decided to put you in mat class during our morning session," he said. "This will help you build up some much needed upper body strength. Classes begin at 10:30, only a few minutes from now. Just wait here, and I'll get you when they're ready to start."

As I sat there, I noticed some signs and posters on the walls. Two that caught my eye were "It Hurts So Good" and "No Pain, No Gain." Then Dave came by, and we went to the end of the room, where attendants were rolling out mats to cover a large area of the floor. I watched as the students were lifted out of their wheelchairs and placed on the mats. A few were able to get out of their chairs by themselves. They would lock the chair and fall forward, breaking their fall with their hands. If I tried that, I'd have broken my neck again. I simply didn't have enough strength in my arms to do anything like that—yet. I was lifted out of my chair and placed on the mat with the others.

We were positioned in a circle around the therapist, who sat in the middle on a stool. Then wrist weights were strapped onto us, ranging in weight from one to five pounds. I couldn't even lift the weight of my arms, so they skipped me for now.

For the next hour, the therapist worked us until I thought I would pass out. It wasn't that I was tired; I'd done very little exercise. But we all had to count out loud with the instructor to keep alert and to force more oxygen into our bodies. The hardest part was having to sit on those hard mats for so long—my buttocks and legs were killing me.

Lunch. Back to occupational therapy. More muscle tests. Time again for physical therapy. I prayed there'd be no more mat classes for the day.

"We're going to do some work on the parallel bars this afternoon," said Dave. That sounded fine to me. ANYTHING but mat class. Pulling my wheelchair up to the bars, I was ready to begin.

For an hour, I worked on standing and walking. Then Dave helped me on one of the bench mats. Strapping ankle weights onto me, he showed me some exercises to do to strengthen my legs. This lasted until 4:30.

After dinner, I had a chance to rest and reflect on all that I had seen that day. I wasn't at the top of the scale—there were many people who had much more control and strength than I had. But I wasn't at the bottom either.

There was a young girl of 19. One night she had been drinking and smoking marijuana with some friends. They climbed a neighbor's fence to go swimming in the pool. Eager to be the first one in, she climbed the high diving board and dove in. She hit the bottom head first—the neighbor had drained all the water from the pool. Her neck was broken, her spinal cord severed. Paralyzed from the neck down, all she could do was talk and move her shoulders slightly.

There was a young man who'd been in an automobile accident. Both of his legs were amputated above the knee. Another man had reacted to the swine flue vaccine. It had affected his spinal cord to such a degree that he was almost completely paralyzed. Tragedy had struck so many. It made me realize that I was not the only one with a problem.

These people's handicaps were real, but many of us have imagined or mental handicaps that are just as debilitating. Whether real or imagined, handicaps can be overcome. They can be seen as tremendous assets or awesome liabilities. It's a matter of attitude.

Despite being deaf and blind, Helen Keller lectured and led an active life as an author and educator. Robert Louis Stevenson was an invalid for the last 20 years of his life, suffering intense pain and high fevers from an incurable case of tuberculosis. Yet he gave us literary gems such as *Treasure Island,* *The Strange Case of Dr. Jekyll and Mr. Hyde,* and *A Child's Garden of Verse.*

Joni Eareckson is a glowing example of how determination and faith can overcome the most severe handicaps. At 17, Joni had broken her neck in a diving accident and was paralyzed from the neck down. Joni had to overcome her mental handicaps of hopelessness and despair—her physical condition is permanent. Now she sketches and paints, holding her artist's tools in her teeth, and travels so that she can tell others how she has grown emotionally and spiritually from her tragedy.

Most people never have to face such major handicaps. But they have built mental barriers to success, happiness, peace of mind, and fulfillment, barriers that can be just as limiting. A circus elephant tied to a stake does not try to pull up the stake because he believes that he cannot. As a baby elephant, he really couldn't budge that stake, so he just stopped trying. People do the same thing. They try, they fail, and then they give up. Sometimes they stop trying new things because their fear of failure is so great. They avoid failure like the plague instead of seeing it as a natural event—a learning process necessary for achieving anything worthwhile in life.

Have you ever tried to learn to play an instrument? It takes years of failure—wrong notes, poor rhythm, scratching or blaring or screeching—before you can succeed. Lots of people take music lessons at some time in their lives, but only a few become musicians. The same idea applies to careers, education, sports, and a hundred other activities that make life worth living. If you don't try, you can't succeed.

I was trying with all my might. It would have been easy to let someone feed me. Time after time, I tried to get a fork full of food all the way to my mouth and failed. But I didn't give up. It would have been easy to accept a lifetime in a wheelchair. The exercises were painful, and I felt foolish. Here I was, a grown man, unable to take three steps without assistance. But I went to therapy and tried harder each day. I may fail 1,000 times, I told myself, but in the end, I will succeed.

The rest of the week was devoted to adjusting to my new environment. Most of the day was spent in therapy. There were more muscle and sensation tests in occupational therapy and morning mat class and work on the parallel bars in physical therapy. I was becoming more comfortable with the staff and students.

One thing I missed was socializing with a roommate. There were several wards in the hospital, referred to as units. Because Unit Two, for spinal cord students, was full when I arrived, I was temporarily in Unit One, for the brain injured. My roommates couldn't speak and were unaware of their surroundings, so I couldn't really get to know them.

It wasn't all that bad, though. I was busy most of the day, and after supper I rested, watched television, listened to my motivational tapes, and concentrated on getting better.

Saturday was a different story. There was no therapy on weekends, half the staff was off, many students went home to their families for the weekend; suddenly it was very lonesome. By evening, I was going crazy from the boredom.

Fortunately, I got a new roommate on Sunday. And he could talk! Ron, who was only 24, had been in an automobile accident about eight years earlier. Because of a spinal cord injury, he had been paralyzed from the waist down and had only limited use of his arms and hands. But there was nothing wrong with his speech. We started talking about our injuries and where our neck breaks were located. His was at C-5, the fifth cervical vertebrae. When I told him that mine was at C-1 and C-2, he couldn't believe it.

"You're supposed to be dead!" he exclaimed.

"I know," I replied, "but I'm not."

I was glad when Monday morning finally arrived. It was July 13, and all my evaluations were over for now. Today I would start working on the many skills I needed to master before I could function well enough to go home. On Friday afternoon, they'd told me I could expect to leave by March 1982. I had other plans.

Julie met me at occupational therapy. She told me that our immediate goals would be to improve my upper body strength. We would work on this and on increasing my range of motion in the morning. Then in the afternoon, we'd do more exercises for upper body strength as well as practice fine motor coordination and hand/finger dexterity skills.

She led me to a huge, black cast-iron machine that looked like an old-time printing press. That's exactly what it was. It had been rigged with cables and weights for use as an exercise machine. Because I didn't have enough strength in my hands to grip the handles, Julie put gloves on my hands and then strapped them to the handles using Ace bandages. There were 24 weights, each weighing about two pounds.

"We'll start you out with two weights," Julie said. "If that's too easy, we can add more." Pushing down to lift the weights, I did four sets of ten without too much trouble.

Next we went to a machine called a sander. This consisted of a wooden box with handles on each side and a piece of sandpaper attached to the bottom. The box sat on a flat wooden board about six inches wide. I was placed in front of the box, which sat on a table, and my hands were wrapped onto the handles. Then Julie put a five-pound weight inside the box. The object was to push the box as far forward as you could, then pull it back again. As you developed more strength, more weights could be added, and the plane of the board could be raised in 10° increments until it was straight up. I managed to do ten sets of five before my arms gave out.

There it was time for physical therapy. I had to suffer through another session of mat class; I was really starting to hate this. I just couldn't see that it was doing me any good. I'll try until Friday, then talk to my counselor, I told myself. There were so many other things I could be doing that *would* help. I just couldn't afford to waste any recovery time.

After lunch, I returned to occupational therapy and did more upper body exercises. An hour later, I followed Julie to a row of tables, where about six people were sitting. Here I was given two projects to work on. The first was a board with holes for plastic pegs, identical to the one I'd used at The Towers. This task was still difficult for me, but not as bad as the next activity.

There was a box of wooden pieces of various shapes and sizes. These had to be matched with the slots on a board. I couldn't keep my grip on the pieces long enough to get them into the slots because of my lack of hand strength and barely functional eye-hand coordination. I did get a few in, but it was no piece of cake. It was hard to believe that something that looked so easy could be so difficult.

When I arrived at physical therapy, Dave was waiting for me.

"Today we're going to try something new," he said. He went to the corner of the room, then returned with two odd-looking walking canes. They were made of metal and had four prongs on the bottom that were covered with rubber stops.

"We call these quad canes," he explained. "Have you ever tried to use these?" I said I hadn't, so we gave them a try. Strapping a belt around my waist, Dave helped me to my feet and placed a cane on each side of me. I gripped them as best I could. My attempts to take steps seemed futile. I would stumble and lose my balance, Dave would catch me, and we would start all over again. We tried the canes for an hour without much progress.

Dave put them back and brought me a walker. Much like an infant's device, it was a metal frame with wheels. This was easier to use. I could actually take a few steps on my own. But the canes involved more skills required for walking unassisted than this rolling support system.

"Don't get discouraged," Dave told me. "We'll try the quad canes again, and you'll get the hang of them." His optimistic attitude was a real morale booster after such a long and strenuous day. Heading for supper, I realized that walking on my own would be my number one goal for a long time.

chapter 8

TAKING THE GOOD
WITH THE BAD

*"There is nothing either good or bad, but
thinking makes it so.*

SHAKESPEARE, *HAMLET*

Hospital routines are a blessing and a curse. Every morning, the staff would come in to help me dress and shave, and they'd bring in my breakfast. They did not let me rot. Every Monday through Friday, I went to therapy, knowing that I would put in a good day's work. Every evening, I knew that I had a few hours to rest and gather my thoughts before getting some much needed sleep. Every weekend, I could relax, listen to my tapes, and socialize. The sameness was driving me crazy.

I got intense pleasure out of anything new—a new exercise in therapy, a new roommate, a new game to play for recreation. Confinement in an institution, no matter how good that institution is, makes you realize the number of options you once had and always took for granted. Unfortunately, the heightened pleasure I received was countered by disappointments that seemed devastating. It took all my concentration and willpower to control these extremes and keep them from swamping me so that I could stay my course to recovery without capsizing.

By the end of my second week, I was becoming more comfortable with my new surroundings. Several of my friends from The Towers were transferred to Woodrow Wilson, and I'd met a lot of new people.

On Saturday, July 18, a young man named Terry Moore arrived. He became one of my closest friends. Terry, a man in his early twenties, was from East Stone Gap, Virginia. His neck had been broken at C-5 and C-6 in an automobile accident. Though paralyzed from the neck down, Terry always seemed to be in good spirits. He and Kenny Williams were rooming together in the only room with two beds I knew of—other rooms had four beds.

Kenny and Terry made a fine pair. They were always joking and kidding around. Most of the time, their jests revolved around a nice-looking young nurse named Frances Jones, who went by the name of Dino. She'd met Kenny at the University of Virginia Hospital in Charlottesville, where she was working as a student nurse. They had kept in touch while Kenny was at The Towers, and now she would come to visit him at Woodrow. Naturally, Terry got to know her, too.

They now both had a crush on her. There were constant, goodnatured arguments about whose girl she was, and I, being an agitator, would add fuel to the fire. When I saw Kenny by himself, I'd tell him stories about Terry and Dino. When I saw Terry, I'd tell him stories about Kenny and Dino. Of course, none of the stories were true. Sometimes I'd get so tickled at the two of them, I'd have to leave the room so that I wouldn't break down and let them in on my little game. This diversion from the harsh reality of our situation helped to ease the loneliness and boredom, especially on weekends.

When the end of the month arrived, I was pleased to see that I'd made some progress in both physical and occupational therapy. Dave had decided that mat class wasn't helping me— thank goodness! So most of my physical therapy time was spent focusing on learning to walk. I just kept visualizing myself walking like a healthy person as I struggled to take a few steps at a time. In occupational therapy, I was gaining more upper body strength, hand and finger dexterity, and was improving my coordination. My recovery was not going by leaps and bounds, but at least it was going—forward.

The doctors believed that my goal of walking on my own, not to mention my goal of complete recovery, was unrealistic. Someone in my condition had never done it before, they reasoned, so I should not hope for the impossible. I refused to believe that a goal had to be accomplished before it could be considered. Roger Bannister, the runner, came to mind.

For over 50 years, mile runners had been trying to run a mile in four minutes. But doctors everywhere had said that it was physically impossible. They claimed that the human body could not stand such a strain—blood vessels would burst, and the heart would rupture. Everyone had been SNIOP'ed into believing that it just couldn't be done.

Along came Roger Bannister. He refused to believe what the doctors had said and what everyone else believed. So one day in 1954, he ran the mile in less than four minutes. But that's only half the story. Sure, it was great that Bannister did the "impossible." What's interesting, though, is that within a year over 30 other runners also broke the record. Not only did Bannister break the record, but he also broke the mental barriers for others. He made the impossible possible.

Andrew Carnegie, the industrial magnate, was the son of a handloom weaver. His dreams did not stop once he had amassed his fortune. A strong believer in man's responsibility to share his wealth and abundance with others, he dreamed of creating opportunity for all and increasing man's knowledge. By 1915, four years before he died, he'd given away $300 million to support education, public libraries, and world peace. He believed that any idea held strongly enough in the mind would express itself.

Bobby Kennedy said it best. In the eulogy Ted Kennedy gave for his brother, he quoted Bobby: "Some men see things as they are and say why. I dream things that never were and say why not."

I had a dream—full recovery. Medical experts have stated that nerves in the spinal cord will not regenerate. However, I am convinced that the human body has the capacity to make new neurological connections to replace damaged nerves. My purpose in striving for a seemingly hopeless goal was twofold: I wanted to do it for myself so that I would not have to spend the rest of my life in a nursing home as a vegetable; and I wanted to do it for others, to clear a pathway so that others would have the courage to strive for their dreams, no matter what the odds. The path I was taking was covered with brambles and thorns, but I continued on.

On Saturday morning, August 1, I awoke with incredible pains in my head. The screws that held my halo to my head had worked themselves loose. Every movement, no matter how small, caused the weight of the heavy metal bars on my head to shift, jabbing the screws into my skull like ice picks.

When I told the head nurse about my problem, a major one as far as I was concerned, she said that there was nothing she could do. Most of the doctors had gone for the weekend, but there was one scheduled to visit that afternoon. She promised that she would bring my difficulty to his attention.

He finally got around to me sometime after supper. After

a brief look at my halo, he said I would have to have the screws tightened.

"We'll send you to Charlottesville on Monday to see Dr. Whitehill," he said.

"Can't you do it now?" I pleaded. "I don't think I can make it until Monday." He insisted that this was completely out of his field, and that I'd just have to hang in there.

He prescribed a mild painkiller, but it didn't do one bit of good. By Sunday morning, I was in a terrible mood. I think that the nurses were surprised to see me this way. Since I'd arrived at Woodrow, I'd always smiled and been happy-go-lucky. Now I was really hurting—the heck with appearances.

I couldn't sleep. If I rested on my right side, the screw would press into my skull; as soon as I turned over, my left side would hurt; lying flat, the screws on the back of my head would dig into me. So I began to watch the clock, counting down the hours until Monday morning. I was going to Charlottesville on Monday, even if I had to crawl the entire way.

The medication they gave me to help me sleep did about as much good as the painkiller. Monday morning at 6:00, I was wide awake when a staffer came to help me dress. By now, the screws were so loose that the entire contraption rattled everytime I moved.

At 8:30, two nurses and four students, one of them me, piled into a compact station wagon and headed for Charlottesville. The trip took us an hour. When we arrived, my arms and legs were numb from being packed like a sardine.

It was another two hours before I got to see Dr. Whitehill. When it was my turn, though, he wasted no time. With wrench in hand, he began tightening the screws down. I thought for sure I was going to pass out. Blood was flowing from the screw points as he finished, and my head felt as if it were about to come off. I almost wished it would!

"That ought to hold you for a while," said Dr. Whitehill. "I tried to make them as tight as I could so they won't come loose for a long time."

You sure did, I thought to myself. If you'd made them any tighter, my skull would have split open.

The ride back to Fishersville was a little more comfortable because one of the students had been admitted to the University

Hospital. Her nurse was still with us, though, so we still had five in a car designed for four.

It was almost 1:00 P.M. before we got back to Woodrow. I didn't feel up to physical therapy—I didn't even feel up to eating lunch! All I wanted to do was lie down and try to sleep. And that's exactly what I did. By Tuesday evening, I finally started to feel human again.

By Wednesday morning, I was doing fairly well, except for a dull throb in my head, so I went with the mat class to the gym for what Dave called wheelchair sports. The gym was in another building. It was a good distance away, and I had quite a struggle pulling myself along, but I made it.

Once everyone had arrived, Dave divided us into two teams.

"We're going to play wheelchair soccer," he announced. The basketball court had been sectioned off by black lines, and we used a beach ball instead of a hard soccer ball.

Because of my limited mobility and arm movement, I was chosen as the goalie. We'd only been playing a short time when the other team got the ball and headed for our goal. Two of their players grabbed my chair to pull me out of the way. The next thing I knew, I was falling forward. My face hit the floor. The impact knocked me silly.

"Are you okay?" asked Dave worriedly. I was dazed, but I told him that I thought I'd be all right. As I watched the other students continue to play, I shook my head in disbelief. Just as I was getting over having my screws tightened, something like this had to happen.

During lunch, one of the other students who'd been in the game was sitting by me.

"You're a tough fellow," he remarked. "I think you must be made of iron."

Well, I'm tough, but I'm not stupid, I wanted to say. There'd be no more soccer for me, if I could help it. The fall in the bus, and now this—I wasn't going to risk breaking my neck again. Once was more than enough, thank you.

I pushed myself to the limit in therapy during the next week. I wanted to make up for the time I'd lost because of my halo coming loose and my fall playing soccer. Besides, the faster I progressed, the sooner I could go home.

In occupational therapy, I could really see an improvement in my right hand. The exercises I had been working on required finer motor skills. But my left hand still wasn't functional. My entire left side was very weak, and I suffered from spasms. Sometimes my left arm and foot would shake so badly that I thought they'd fall off. I was put on Baclafin to help control the spasms, but I didn't see any noticeable improvement.

In physical therapy, I had practiced enough with the walker so that I could get around fairly well. But I still couldn't grasp the quad canes well enough to have much success with them. To repeat the old saying: "It's hard by the yard, but a cinch by the inch." My inches weren't such cinches, but yards would have been too much to expect at this stage.

Saturday, August 8, started out just as any other weekend. After lunch, I was visiting Terry and Kenny, when we got onto the subject of food. We all agreed that it would be nice to have something really good for a change.

"It sure would be nice to have a pizza," said Terry.

"Let's get one then," I replied. They thought I was kidding, but I was dead serious.

I headed out to the nurses station and asked if I could use the phone. Although it was not usually permitted, they told me to go ahead. Then I asked one of the nurses to look in the Yellow Pages for me and give me the number of a pizza parlor. Next I got the number of a cab company. The nurse looked rather surprised when I actually called the pizza place and ordered a large pizza, then called the cab company and asked them to pick it up and deliver it to us.

That pizza ended up costing us about $20. It was worth every penny. Terry, Kenny, and I devoured that pizza in nothing flat. We probably could have eaten another one! From then on, almost every weekend was pizza weekend.

Sometimes during the week, I'd call a cab and have them go to Arby's to get me a roast beef sandwich and potato cakes. Most of the time, the food at Woodrow was okay, not what you'd call down-home cooking, but not bad for institutional food. But when there was something on the menu that I just didn't care for, I would call a cab and order something from town. Terry's desire for a pizza really started something. Ordering out for food became one of those little pleasures that meant so much.

On Monday morning, I was told that I had an appointment with Dr. Whitehill in Charlottesville the next day. I'd have some new X-rays taken, and if the fusion in my neck looked good, they'd take off my halo. No more screws to work loose, I thought excitedly. I'd been looking forward to this for a long time. If I could get rid of this thing on my head, maybe I'd feel like a healthy person again.

When physical therapy ended that afternoon, my counselor, Duane, asked me to meet him in his office for a few minutes.

"I know you're looking forward to your visit tomorrow," he said.

"I sure am," I replied.

"Just don't get your hopes up too high," he cautioned. "I've seen many people go expecting to have their halo removed only to find that it would be awhile longer." Deep down I knew he was right, that I was setting myself up for quite a fall if things didn't go well. But I didn't think I could stand it much longer. For sanity's sake, I had to believe that tomorrow I would have one of my dreams come true. That night I convinced myself that if it didn't come off, I could make it for another week or two—just in case.

Six to eight weeks! Dr. Whitehill was saying that my neck wasn't healing as fast as he'd anticipated; it would need more time to fuse; he'd check me again in six to eight weeks. I saw his mouth moving and heard the words coming out, but they wouldn't register. It was as if I were in a mental fog. This must be a terrible nightmare—I'd wake up, and everything would be fine. But it wasn't. It was time to face reality.

The disappointment was almost too much to bear. When I returned to Woodrow Wilson, I went straight to bed. Again, I couldn't push myself to go to therapy. After my screws were tightened, just two weeks ago, I had been in physical pain. Now I was in mental anguish.

That day I did a lot of thinking. Lately, I'd been on an emotional roller coaster. Good things were great, bad things were horrible—or were they? Maybe it was just my perception of these events. Somehow, I'd gotten away from my mental health program of positive thinking. It was time for a pep talk.

Okay, Morris, I told myself, think about how much you've been through and how much you've accomplished. You're alive! Are you going to let a minor setback like this halo thing ruin your progress? At least you can look forward to it coming off; all that metal they put in your neck is doing some good. So what if you can't put those pegs in the holes too well yet. It'll get better.

And there's nothing wrong with getting excited about a pizza. But just think—once you're home, you can have pizza whenever you want without calling a cab!

I suddenly realized that I'd allowed myself to start building mental spider webs. The spider web of disappointment was draining me of my energy and hope, catching my drive and position attitude like unsuspecting flies. I'd come too far to let this happen now.

By the time I went to sleep that night, I was feeling much better. On Wednesday morning, I came up with a plan.

chapter **9**

HOME BY CHRISTMAS

"Never give in, never, never, never, never."

WINSTON CHURCHILL

I had had a close call with that halo incident. Satan's wedge of discouragement had almost done its job. But I had caught myself before I lost my momentum. Now I was more determined than ever to recover and get back home. I didn't give in—to despair, to frustration, to taking the easy road. I was my old self again, raring to go and resolved to work harder than ever.

Starting tomorrow, August 13, I would get up one hour earlier, at 5:30, so that I could be in occupational therapy by 7:30—one hour earlier than the therapists so that I'd have the whole place to myself. There were lots of details to work out with the staff about my routines. The people who dressed me in the morning, the nurses, and the therapists all had to be consulted. But everyone cooperated. From that day on, I was the first person in therapy in the morning and the last to leave at the end of the day.

My new schedule helped me boost my morale, focus my energy on constructive efforts, and feel better about myself. It also helped others. Seeing people try harder or start to try again, because they were influenced by my example, gave me a good feeling. Knowing that others relied on me for encouragement made me work all the harder.

On Monday morning, while I was in therapy, Duane Anderson walked in.

"I'd like to see you this afternoon," he told me. Well, whether it was good news or bad news, I was going to handle it. It turned out to be a little bit of both.

"How would you like to go home for an entire week?" he asked me after I had entered his office. Before I could say anything, he told me that he'd already spoken with Sandy, and things were tentatively set for next week.

A million questions raced through my head. Being home for the weekend had been difficult back in July. I envisioned all sorts of problems. But I'd made some progress since then, and I could use a break, a chance to recharge my batteries before I made the final push. The staff had set a projected release date of March 1982. I planned to be home by Christmas. That would mean long days of intensive therapy sessions. A change of scenery would do me good. Still, I had my doubts. Could Sandy stand the stress of caring for me for so many days in a row?

Duane sensed my turmoil.

"You'll come back with a new-found spirit and strength to make it the rest of the way," he assured me. "And this will give you and us a chance to see firsthand the problems you'll face out in the real world."

We both knew that Woodrow Wilson was a make-believe fantasy world. Everything was designed with the handicapped person in mind. The floors were tiled and level. There were no curbs to contend with. Water fountains were at wheelchair level, and so were the telephones. In fact, the telephones had special attachments that held the receiver close to your ear without requiring the use of hands. Things just weren't like this on the outside, but it was time to try my wings.

"Let's call Sandy," Duane said. He dialed the number and handed the telephone to me. With some uncertainty, Sandy agreed to give it a try. If my sister, Pat, could make it, they'd drive up together on Friday morning, August 28, to get me. I could return anytime before Sunday, September 6.

The staff at Woodrow Wilson was extremely supportive. There was no stigma attached to being handicapped. If you couldn't perform a necessary task in the usual way, they tried to devise a new way. But the staff wasn't soft, either. You were expected to work—hard. And you were expected to follow the rules.

Rules of conduct included the prohibition of drinking, using abusive language, fighting, fraternizing with the opposite sex in their rooms or yours, drugs, and other restrictions designed to protect all students. Each student was given a handbook of these rules upon admittance, and then a counselor went over them to make sure that there were no misunderstandings. A violation meant termination of your stay—no questions asked.

On Wednesday, August 19, a friend of mine broke the rules. He was caught smoking marijuana. The staff was true to its word, and he was told that he would be terminated on Friday. What a shame! He'd been making pretty good progress in therapy and really needed the help he was receiving, but now that would all come to an end.

The message in these rules was clear. Don't waste your time and ours, taking up valuable space, by escaping from your problems. If you try to do the best that you can, if you try to meet the challenge, we will help you as much as we can. But if you give up or give in, don't expect *us* to keep trying.

Thursday, August 27, is a day I will never forget. My extra hours of therapy were paying off. I was gaining strength and coordination in my hands and fingers. Buttoning shirts, tying shoes, brushing teeth, and writing were all skills still beyond my abilities, but I was certain that these would come with practice. In physical therapy, I was getting around quite well in my walker. That doesn't mean that in a race with a turtle, I would have come in first, but at least I was moving around in an upright position.

Well, that day as I wheeled into physical therapy, Dave was busy with another student.

"I'll be back with you in a few minutes," he said. When he'd finished, he came to me with a smile on his face.

"Are you ready to walk?" he asked me.

"Sure," I told him.

"Okay, stand up and let's go," he said.

"Where's my walker?" I wanted to know.

"I don't think you need it," Dave answered. "Let's try without it."

If Dave thought that I was ready, I was willing to give it a try—I had a lot of confidence in him. He stood beside me holding onto the waist of my pants, and I started off. My sense of balance was still messed up, and I wobbled all over the place, but I did take a few steps. Those steps made me feel as if I'd broken the four-minute mile with Roger Bannister! I felt an enormous sense of accomplishment. What news for Sandy and Pat when they arrive tomorrow, I thought. I was looking forward to my trip home, and now this. I was bursting at the seams.

At 11:00 Sandy and Pat arrived, and I was ready to roll. The night before, a nurse had helped me pack everything I needed. But before I left, I wanted to introduce Julie and Dave to my family and give a demonstration of what I'd been working on in therapy.

During our meeting with Dave, Sandy expressed her concern about my falling if I tried to walk. Dave assured her that as long as I used my walker and took my time, the chance of my falling was about one in a million. Pat seemed satisfied with Dave's assurances and told Sandy not to worry, but there was doubt written all over my wife's face. Unaccustomed to my routines and uncertain of my abilities, it wasn't surprising that Sandy should be hesitant to take on such a burden of responsibility.

It was almost 12:30 before we got into the car. None of us had eaten lunch, and we were all hungry.

"Do you want to stop somewhere and have lunch?" Pat asked.

"Why don't we stop at the Howard Johnson's just a few miles up the road?" I answered.

That suited everyone, and a few minutes later, we pulled into the parking lot. With my walker for support, I hobbled into the restaurant. You probably know what I ordered—a grilled cheese sandwich and an orange freeze! I threw in an order of french fries for good measure. It was my old standby diet, with a difference. Here I was, out in public, eating a meal like a normal human being.

Soon we were back on the road and heading for home. My mother was going to have dinner ready and waiting for us when we arrived so that we could all sit down and relax after our long trip. The ride home seemed much longer than it was. My legs and buttocks were burning like fire. And then there was the problem of urinating.

I had decided not to wear a leg bag. Instead, I would use a bottle. We planned to make frequent rest stops so that I could get out, stretch my legs, and relieve myself. About two hours into our trip, I felt the urge to urinate. I tried to use the bottle, but I had no luck. At the next rest stop, I hobbled inside with my walker. My bladder just wouldn't work. I got back in the car, and we were off again.

Every hour I would get the urge to go, but the results were always the same. This worried me. The doctors had warned me that if such a problem developed and continued, it was a sign that the entire system was about to break down. I was told that this happened fairly often with spinal cord patients and required immediate hospitalization.

I told Pat and Sandy that before panicking we should wait until we got to Mother's to see if things got better by then. It seemed as if we'd never get there. As soon as we arrived, I got into the house as fast as I could. We all waited anxiously until finally, after 15 minutes of straining, I succeeded. For the time being, we could all breathe a sign of relief, but I knew that this was something I'd have to keep a close watch on.

After supper Sandy and I got back into the station wagon and headed for our home in Virginia Beach. Pat followed in her car to help us get organized. We anticipated a busy weekend, but, despite our best efforts, it was very late before the lights were out for the night.

Friends who'd missed me during my last stay at home were eager to see me. All my relatives wanted to stop in for a visit. And Sandy's mom and dad were planning to arrive on Saturday afternoon for a week-long stay. It had been awhile since I'd seen Mom and Dad, so I was really looking forward to seeing them. There are a lot of jokes about how rotten in-laws can be—but not mine. They couldn't have been dearer to me if they had been my own parents.

As expected, on Saturday the house looked like a shopping mall during the holiday season. Again, I felt the warm glow of contentment that comes from knowing that so many friends and relatives are willing to stick by you, even during the most difficult of times.

By 4:30 when Mom and Dad arrived, everyone had gone. We all sat down to a delicious dinner of fresh fish, mashed potatoes, coleslaw, string beans, and iced tea, which Sandy had lovingly prepared. Woodrow Wilson might have wonderful therapy equipment, but it just couldn't compete with a home-cooked meal. It was almost midnight before we finished catching up on what had happened since our last visit, and went to bed.

Ah! The smell of scrambled eggs and toast! A week of this might spoil me, I thought. Maybe I won't go back. But that was wishful thinking. There was much more therapy to complete before I could handle living in the real world full-time.

Sunday was another house-full-of-company day. Sharing

a few laughs and stories with old friends helped ease the pain that constantly reminded me of my condition. These weekend visitors were the best therapy in the world.

My week at home was passing much too quickly. Before I knew it, it was Thursday. I was going to get a haircut and a manicure today. My stylist for several years, Lori Baker, was going to see what she could do with my shaggy mop. My hair was so long and matted that I had serious doubts about it ever looking as it used to.

When she had finished and I looked in the mirror, I could hardly believe my eyes. A member of the human race stared back at me from the glass. Wait until I get back to Woodrow, I chuckled. No one will recognize me.

Then a manicurist did my fingernails. Before the accident, I'd always done my own manicures: trimming the nails, pushing the cuticles back, and then buffing the nails to a high gloss. I couldn't do any of this by myself now. With my hair and nails done, I felt like a million dollars. Mom and Dad were pleasantly shocked at the difference a few hours of help could make.

Thursday was my last night home. We'd decided that I'd return to Woodrow on Friday. Mom, Dad, and Sandy would be making the trip with me. Dad was having problems with the circulation in his legs, and I thought the trip would be too much for him. But he insisted on driving me back.

That night, try as I might, I couldn't sleep. There was so much to think about—mostly the week's stay at home and what was coming up at Woodrow for my last push toward rehabilitation. My family and I had tried to function like a normal family unit, but deep down I had felt that it was mostly pretending. I required so much care. There were so many things that I couldn't do for myself. Would any of our lives ever be normal again, I wondered.

Once I returned to therapy, I planned to push myself to the limit every day. If I was going to meet my self-imposed deadline of getting home for good by Christmas, I had only four months to retrain nearly every one of my muscles. Compounding the problem were hundreds of short circuits in my neurological system.

And then there was Sandy. The love and tenderness, the home-cooked meals and homey atmosphere—everything that represented a happy married life—I would have to leave again. I tried to console myself. The tears of today would become the smiles and laughter of a lifetime. I must steel myself for the long, hard campaign ahead. I must concentrate all of my energies on the present so that the future would fulfill my dreams.

Shortly after my crash, one doctor had told me that the odds for my recovery were a million to one. If a bookie were taking bets on this fight, the odds would have been astronomical. But the trip home had been a welcome break, and now I was ready to begin the battle for my freedom.

We awoke the next morning before daybreak. Dad wanted to leave no later than 8:00 so that we'd have time to stop for lunch and still arrive at Woodrow between 2:30 and 3:00. Everyone wanted to know why I was so quiet. The truth was that my mind was still on the previous night's thoughts, but I told them I was just tired.

After stopping at the Howard Johnson's in Charlottesville, we arrived at the rehab center and started to unload the car. Eager to get back on the road so that they'd reach home by midnight, my family was ready to go as soon as I was settled in. I knew Dad was tired from the trip, but I just had to introduce him to Dave and Julie and show him what I'd been working on. After a very brief demonstration and some questions, Dad was visibly chomping at the bit, so we cut things short.

We all hugged and kissed each other goodbye, and then they left. As I stood at the window and watched them pull away, I felt as if part of me was leaving with them. I was on my own again. The sooner I got down to business and recovered, the sooner the rest of me could leave, too—forever.

On Saturday morning, September 5, I read a notice on the bulletin board that said John Cordle, my old friend from The Towers, would be checking in on Monday. This was great news.

John was supposed to have been at Woodrow a week before my arrival. He'd checked out of The Towers on a Friday, the same as I had, and had gone home for the weekend. That Monday, his wife was supposed to bring him to Woodrow for admittance. John refused to go. Several weeks later, he had had a change of heart, but the Woodrow staff wouldn't let him off the hook that easily. They were still mad about what he'd done.

Now, he was finally coming. I was glad for him because I knew that he'd get a lot of help at Woodrow—not only physical but also mental—to help him cope with his disability.

One of my roommates had been discharged, so there was a vacant bed. On Saturday night, I asked Jean, the head nurse, if she could arrange for John to be assigned to my room. She promised to do whatever she could. When I returned from therapy on Monday afternoon, there were John and his wife, Mozelle. Boy, were they surprised to see me!

"I'll bet you had something to do with this," Mozelle commented.

"I sure did," I answered. "I arranged the whole thing."

That evening after Mozelle had left, John and I caught up on what had been happening since we had last seen each other. He was particularly concerned about the negative rumors he'd heard about Woodrow. I assured him that, from what I had seen during my stay, they were totally unfounded. John knew that I didn't pull any punches. If there were problems, I'd tell him the truth. I had put his fears to rest, and John slept peacefully that night.

The next Saturday, September 12, I had another talk with the head nurse, Jean.

"I need another favor," I told her.

"What's that?" she asked.

"I need to get on a regular schedule for my bath and shampoo," I pleaded. Up until then, these necessary duties were done whenever they could fit me in.

"Would it be possible to have a bath and get my hair washed three times a week?" I requested in my sweetest tone of voice. This was a compromise, since I'd washed my hair, which is very oily, every day before the accident. Anything was better than nothing, though, and I didn't want to push my luck.

To my delight, Jean readily agreed. Maybe she could see how much better I felt since I'd had a haircut. When I became a normal person again, I certainly wanted to look the part. Well, whether it was out of pity or friendliness, she said that the staff would take on this rather difficult set of chores. Every Tuesday, Thursday, and Saturday, they helped me out of my wheelchair and onto a stretcher. Then I would lie on my back with my head hanging over one end. This position made it easier for them to get to my hair and body without so much interference from my halo. They weren't professionals like Lori back in Virginia Beach, but I must admit, they did a fine job on my hair. Keeping my appearance as neat as possible was my reward to myself for working so hard in therapy. Little things can make a difference!

I was now gaining control over some basic bodily functions. My bladder was working with regularity, so I was able to urinate on my own. This meant that I didn't have to wear a leg bag. When I had to go to the bathroom, I simply slid to the edge of the bed, transferred into my wheelchair, and wheeled myself into the bathroom.

Several of the nurses had warned me about the risks of this practice. They told me that I should ask for help when I needed to get out of bed—just ring the bell and someone would come. I realized that this advice was for my own good, but each day gave me increased confidence that I could do it on my own. I should have listened to them.

On Sunday night, September 15, about 10:00, I felt the urge to go to the bathroom. I sat up, slid to the edge of the bed, and went right over the side. I'd lost my balance and fell face forward onto the floor. My forehead hit a metal trash can with such force that it put a dent in the container the size of a half dollar. The two metal prongs on the back of my halo caught in the bed railing and were twisting my neck to one side. Blood was running out of my nose like a river. My neck ached so badly that I was sure I'd broken it again.

I yelled as loud as I could. Between the screaming and all the noise I'd made falling out of bed, John woke up and rang for a nurse. Three nurses and two aides came running into the room. It took all five of them to lift me up and get my halo untangled from the railing. Once I was back in bed, Wanda, the charge nurse, returned with an ice pack.

"Let's put this over your nose until the bleeding stops," she said. "I think it might be broken." My nose was swollen, my eyes were turning black, and I was hurting so badly that I needed a sleeping pill to get some rest that night.

The next morning, I was taken to a doctor in Staunton to have my nose examined. Sure enough, I'd broken it. At the time of my accident last March, a broken nose had been the least of my worries. Now, when things were going so well, it was really annoying, not to mention painful.

By noon I was back at Woodrow, and I took a short nap. I woke up at 1:15, and even though I didn't really feel up to therapy, I decided to go. Maybe if I kept busy, I could keep my mind off of the ache in the middle of my face.

Nearly everyone had some funny comment about my swollen nose and black eyes. When Dave first saw me, he took a hard look and commented, "I see you've been fighting with the nurses."

"No," I replied, "just with a stubborn trash can." He looked puzzled, and I told him I'd explain later. "Let's get to work so I can get out of this place before I accidentally kill myself." As if nothing had happened, we worked on my walking for the afternoon.

In therapy on Tuesday, I saw a friend, Dave Walker. Somehow he looked different, but I couldn't put my finger on it. Finally, after about 20 minutes, it sank in.

"You got a haircut," I said.

"I sure did," he answered. "How do you like it?"

I had to admit that someone had done a pretty good job. I asked around and found out from the nurses that there was a resident barber at Woodrow, but everyone said that he wasn't very good. Most of the students preferred to avoid what they called the "resident butcher."

"Where did you get your haircut?" I finally asked Dave. "Did you go to the barber here?"

"Heavens, no," came the reply. "A lady hair stylist by the name of Nancy Cunningham did it last night. She comes here about once a week to cut and style hair."

I could hardly wait for therapy to end. Before going to lunch, I went straight to the nurses station to ask about having my hair cut and styled on a regular basis. I was told that she was coming in that night! The woman at the desk said that she'd call Nancy to see if she could work me into her schedule.

When I returned from therapy that afternoon, there was a note on my bed saying that Nancy would do my hair that night at 8:00. Right on time, she walked in and got to work.

"Can you bend forward over the sink?" she asked.

"I think so," I said. Although it was awkward and put a strain on my neck, I managed to lean over long enough for her to wash my hair. After she had finished clipping and blow-drying my hair, I asked her how much I owed her.

"No charge," said Nancy, but I wouldn't hear of it. I gave her two $10 bills. To me, it was worth every penny. She put one of the tens back into the pouch behind my wheelchair.

"We'll compromise," she stated. "Ten dollars is plenty. Any time you need another haircut, just let Sandy, the woman at the desk, know, and she'll get in touch with me."

"You bet!" I told her. "You can count on me as a regular customer."

In physical therapy, my main emphasis was still on walking and improving my balance. I wasn't too steady on my feet for a number of reasons. First, the weight of all that metal on my head made me top-heavy. Second, there was the problem of my toes. All the toes on my left foot were curled under—it was like my trying to walk on a rubber ball. So far, we hadn't found a way to correct this. My biggest problem, though, was the improper neurological feedback of all of the muscles and nerves on my left side. At the time, however, I wasn't aware of this last difficulty, so I kept plugging away, figuring that it was just something that would improve with practice.

Now that I was getting up earlier, I made it to occupational therapy by 8:00. This gave me some uninterrupted time to work on my upper body strength. The room was dark and empty when I arrived in the morning, but I always went right to work, usually with the printing press machine and the sander. Once the therapists arrived at 8:45, I'd work with Julie on fine motor skills. Writing, typing, stringing beads, picking up buckshot with tweezers, putting washers on screws, assembling puzzles, and putting those little pegs in the board were just some of the activities they'd devised for improving eye-hand coordination and for getting all of the small muscles in the fingers and hands back into shape.

When Friday, September 18, rolled around, I breathed a sigh of relief. It had been a long, tough week, and I was actually looking forward to a quiet, restful weekend. As if by some devious, sinister plan, things were anything but restful.

That night, the screws in my halo became loose again, and I spent the entire weekend in agony. On Monday morning, I was off again to see Dr. Whitehill in Charlottesville. Again, I went through the painful tightening procedure, but this time there was a ray of hope. Dr. Whitehill made an appointment for the following week to have X-rays taken. Perhaps my neck had mended enough to remove the halo for good.

Naturally, I was happy, but I was cautious about getting my hopes up. The last time, I'd felt as if I'd fallen off a cliff. This time I planned on staying closer to the ground so I wouldn't hit so hard when I fell.

Dick Manson, an old friend, paid me a surprise visit on Wednesday. Waiting for my return trip to Charlottesville was driving me crazy, so this pleasant distraction was great. Dick and I had spent countless hours hunting, fishing, flying, and just palling around together over the years.

One experience that we recalled as we chatted that day brought back memories of my crash. In November 1980, just five months before my accident, Dick, a farmer named Tom Smith, and I went on a duck-hunting trip to the Barrier Islands. We decided to fly in and land on the beach instead of taking a boat—the islands are accessible only by water; there are no bridges. Because there is no beach to speak of during high tide, a man named Robert Scott agreed to fly in with us and then fly the plane back to the mainland. Then, six hours later, during the next low tide, Page Scott would land and pick us up.

Because of the short runway, the power lines (the same ones I'd plowed through in March), and being loaded to full capacity with four people and our gear, the takeoff to the Barrier Islands was tricky. We cleared the wires at the last minute, and my passengers were left white and speechless for the rest of the trip. But the day had its lighter moments.

As we were watching a pair of black ducks land in the marsh, Tom suggested that Dick and I try to sneak up on them. I led the way, and Dick followed. Not long after that, I heard all sorts of commotion coming from behind me. Turning around, I saw Dick covered to the waist and sinking fast in a quicksand mire. I quickly headed back to help him. Catching hold of his hand, I gave a mighty tug. Well, Dick came out, but his boots didn't. Then I lost my grip, and we were back to square one. Dick's face was now as black from the mud as it had been white from the fright earlier. With Dick cursing and me tugging, we finally managed to work him out of the mess.

Tom had had quite a show—he'd been watching the whole time. In fact, he was laughing so hard you could have heard him a mile away.

Dick and I shared this story and others for the next three hours, and then it was time for him to go. His visit did wonders for my spirits that day. Getting my mind off the coming big event relaxed me and gave me a boost to get through the next several days. I started thinking about how one day I would once again walk the fields and marshes with good friends, enjoying nature to its fullest.

Today's going to be fun, I thought to myself on Saturday. I'd signed up with the recreation department for bowling. At 10:00 A.M., a student volunteer came to wheel me over to the Recreation Center. I could hardly wait to show my stuff; after all, I'd bowled three super games at The Towers, and now I had more control over my movements.

They set me up with a contraption like the one I'd used before. After carefully lining things up, I let the ball roll down the ramp.

"Right on target!" I said as it headed straight for the head-pin. But I spoke too soon. At the last minute, the ball veered off to the left. Frustrated, I tried again. This time, before the ball reached the pins, it went off to the right.

The problem was with the lanes, not with me—they were warped. I rolled two games and never broke 100. Disappointed, I decided that was the last time I'd bowl on *those* lanes. What was the point of trying if the score had more to do with luck and the shape of the lane than with skill?

Back in my room, getting ready for lunch, I heard a familiar voice: "Where you been, hot shot?" It was Doug Martin. His timing couldn't have been better. I told him all about my bowling adventure and filled him in on my progress. We talked and toured the campus for almost three hours. Once again, a friend had helped me shorten the day and get my mind off my coming trip to Charlottesville.

Finally the day arrived for my visit to Dr. Whitehill's office—Wednesday, September 30. I was awake before daybreak, my anxiety level was at fever pitch. I still had to guard against getting my hopes up too high, but I couldn't help believing that everything would be okay and that today I would get this incapacitating contraption off me.

By 10:00 I was at the doctor's office and ready for my X-rays. Then I had to wait for an hour before they were taken. How much longer will this take? How much more can *I* take?

"Well, everything looks fine," said Dr. Whitehill as he walked through the door. "How would you like to get that thing off your head?" So the suspense was over. Shocked and relieved, I just nodded my head.

He reached into a drawer and took out a wrench—the same type he'd used to tighten the screws three times before. Thank goodness he was loosening them this time.

"This may hurt a little," he cautioned.

"Go right ahead," I quipped. "It can't hurt any worse than when you tighten the screws." I would have gone through any amount of pain to get that thing removed for good.

I was surprised that it took only a matter of minutes, and it didn't bother me at all. As soon as everything was off, my head fell forward. For six months, my neck muscles hadn't been used, so now they were very weak, like a newborn baby's.

"It will take a long time for your neck muscles to build back up," Dr. Whitehill told me. "In the meantime, I'm going to have you fitted for a neck support brace. I want you to wear it at all times until I see you in about five weeks."

I was then wheeled into another room, where a woman fitted me with a brace known as a Philadelphia Collar. A piece of Styrofoam was cut to conform to my neck and chin. The collar was in two parts, which were held together by strips of Velcro, a nylon mesh material with tiny fibers that stick easily to other surfaces. This made it simple to take off and put back on.

The collar made my neck and chin itch like crazy. I would go nuts if I had to put up with this for five weeks straight. Luckily, the nurses back at Woodrow Wilson knew what to do. They lined the inside of the collar with cheesecloth, making the thing bearable. It was still annoying, but in comparison to the halo vest, it was wonderful. Nevertheless, I hadn't anticipated having *anything* on my neck. I had to keep telling myself, you've made it this far, and you can hang in there for a few more weeks.

Now that my halo was off, a new activity was available to me—swimming. Since I'd first laid eyes on the pool during the tour I had while I was still at The Towers, I'd wanted to take a dip. But the rules strictly stated that no students with halos were allowed into the pool. This was because there was a lambswool lining inside the body-cast section of the vest, which cushioned it against my skin. If this got wet, it would be soaked for days. Well, it was gone now, and I was going to have some fun.

Before the accident, I'd been a fairly good swimmer and loved the cool, buoyant feel of the water. So during lunch the very next day, I asked about the swimming schedule. It turned out that there was a swim set for that night. Amy Bridge, who was in charge of recreation, asked me if I'd like to go. I told her I'd be ready and waiting.

That night after supper, I met with some other students in the recreation hall. A volunteer was assigned to each of us, and we were rolled over to the edge of the pool. Then we were helped out of our clothes and into our swimming trunks—mine were very tight around the legs, but I managed to get into them.

My aide helped me into the pool and placed a rubber inner tube over my head and then under my arms to keep me afloat because I couldn't use my arms or legs well enough to swim. The tube put a lot of pressure on my shoulders. This caused pain in my neck. I had expected the cool water to help alleviate the burning sensation in my legs. Instead, it made it worse. Fun time was turning into a torture session.

Our swim lasted for two hours. That was two hours too many. This was to be my first and last time in the pool. When I got back to the hospital, all of the nurses asked me what was wrong. Disappointment must have been written all over my face. I tried to smile, and I told them that I'd enjoyed my swim, but I'm sure they knew better.

The next day when I arrived at physical therapy, Dave said he had a surprise for me.

"I've decided to confiscate your wheelchair and replace it with a walker," he said.

"You can't do that," I replied.

"Why not?" he asked.

"Because it's not one of yours. I bought it when I was at The Towers," I responded. That caught him by surprise, but he recovered quickly.

"Okay," he replied. "But I don't want to see you down here with it, or else I'm going to have to put it in storage until you leave." With that, he took my wheelchair and rolled it back to my room.

When he returned, he gave me a walker.

"This is all yours. From now on I want you to use this to get here and back."

"Okay, I'll give it a go," I told him.

Then Dave told me that he had another surprise in mind, but it would have to wait until the afternoon session. So I struggled through the day with the walker and wondered what else he had in store for me.

At lunchtime, I hobbled back to my room, got into my wheelchair, and went to eat. Then I had to go back to my room, get the walker, and make it back to therapy. By the time I got there, I was huffing and puffing like an old man. Finally the day's session was over, and Dave asked me if I was ready for my second surprise.

"Okay," I said. "Let's hear it."

"Just wait right here for a minute," Dave said. I sat down on one of the benches and watched as Dave went to my walker and left the room with it. He came back in about ten minutes.

"I took it to your room," he informed me. "Now all you have to do is walk back and get it."

"Surely you must be joking," I replied. But he was quite serious.

"Okay, let's go," Dave said. "I'll walk with you." So, with Dave holding onto the waist of my pants, I headed for my room. My destination seemed miles away, but I was determined to make it. Several times I stumbled and lost my balance, but Dave always caught me. We took a lot of rests so that I could catch my breath.

When I arrived at my room, I was soaked in sweat—there wasn't a dry inch of skin on me anywhere. Looking at me, you'd have thought I'd just spent ten hours in the sun doing heavy labor. I fell across my bed like a sack of flour. But there was a smile on my face that no amount of pain and exhaustion could erase.

As I was progressing from a wheelchair to a walker to walking on my own, the seasons were also making their never-ending progression. The hot haze of summer had given way to crystal-clear skies. Almost overnight the landscape had gone from rich, solid greens to an artist's palette covered in yellows, reds, and oranges. The chilly nights hinted at the sparkling snow and bitter cold winds that would soon arrive. The migrating birds reminded me that it was quickly nearing the time for me also to leave this place. Home by Christmas, home by Christmas, I kept chanting to myself.

In therapy, on Monday, October 5, I was waiting for Dave to help me practice my walking when a new student appeared. He was being pushed in a wheelchair by one of the therapists.

"Meet Frankie Campbell," she said, stopping in front of me.

"Hello, Frankie," I said. He looked back at me with a distant look in his eyes.

"How are you doing?" he asked.

"I'm doing fine. How about you?" I asked.

"How are you doing?" he responded.

He kept repeating the same question over and over again. It was all he could say. Frankie had been in a car wreck and had suffered brain damage. That night I learned from one of the nurses that he had a wife and child.

Every time Frankie saw me at mealtime, in the hall, or in therapy, he would come up and ask me the same thing over and over again. It was as if he wanted to have a conversation so much that he went through the motions as best he could. He had the same "conversation" with the other students, the nurses, and the therapists. Many of the students made fun of him. But I felt sorry for Frankie. Before I went to sleep that day of our first meeting, I said a special prayer for Frankie, and once again thanked God for my blessings.

That Wednesday I met with my counselor, Duane, after my therapy session was over. When he made the appointment, he'd told me there was something he needed to discuss with me. I shuffled into the office, sat down, and waited for him to speak.

"I spoke with Meg today," he began. Meg Harris had taken over for Julie, who'd finished her affiliation last week and had returned home. "Meg thinks she's done all she can for you. She wants to discharge you from occupational therapy and send you home. I haven't checked with physical therapy yet, but I plan on talking with Dave in the morning to see what he has to say."

I was visibly shocked. This was a completely unexpected

turn of events. They'd been telling me that I should expect to be discharged in March. I'd been pushing for Christmas. But right now? It was just too soon.

"How do you feel about this?"Duane asked.

"You've really caught me by surprise," I told him. "I don't think I'm ready to go home. I feel that I'm still making progress. And one thing is for sure—Sandy isn't ready yet. She's in the process of selling our home and moving into a townhouse. While I was home, we found a place, but she hasn't moved in yet."

Duane and I agreed to meet again the next afternoon to discuss this in more detail. Meanwhile, he'd talk to Meg and Dave, and I'd call Sandy.

That night I called home. Sandy told me that she'd already started packing and planned on moving in about a week or two. Then it would take another two weeks for her to get things straight. There was just no way I could go home right now.

Armed with that information, I met with Duane the next day, hoping to convince him of how terrible the timing was for such a momentous step. He told me that he'd talked with Meg and Dave, and they'd come to an agreement. Dave felt that I still needed some work in physical therapy, but Meg was sure that I didn't need her help anymore.

The outcome of all of this was a compromise. I would be discharged from occupational therapy, but I could use the equipment on my own. The same thing applied to physical therapy. When the therapists weren't too busy there, though, they would try to work with me.

"We're going to push your discharge forward to November 13," Duane concluded. "I'll call Sandy and go over things with her."

When I walked out of Duane's office that afternoon, I was still shocked. November 13 was only five weeks away. Never in my wildest dreams had I imagined I could be home by Thanksgiving. Chaotic waves of emotion battered my brain with joy and fear, hope and disappointment, while undercurrents of anxiety too fleeting to identify tugged at my self-confidence. Question upon question pounded the beach of my consciousness, then receded, escaping before I could find their answers. One thing was clear: it was going to take me several days before I could regain my concentration and get down to the serious work of learning as much about rehabilitation as I possibly could before I left the sheltered environment of Woodrow for good.

It was about 2:30 on the afternoon of Friday, October 9, when I had a harrowing experience that I would like to forget. I was in therapy, lifting weights. Unable to bench press even ten pounds straight over my head, I was working on a modified bench-press technique. A therapist put me on an incline board, and I would push the barbell up an incline of about 45°. I'd worked up to about 30 pounds since I'd started this exercise. Today I hoped to do five sets of ten. As I finished the third set, a siren went off.

"What's going on?" I asked a therapist as he ran by.

"That's a fire alarm," he shouted. "Let's get outside on the double." Then he was gone.

All of the therapists were scurrying about, lifting people into wheelchairs and pushing them toward the door. People were running about like the proverbial chickens with their heads cut off.

"Someone help get this weight off me!" I hollered as loud as I could. With all the noise, no one seemed to hear me. There I was, powerless to move the weight on my chest because I couldn't raise it enough to crawl out from under it. Finally a therapist saw my plight and yanked it off me.

"Help me out of here!" I pleaded. But before I could finish the sentence, he was gone. Frantic now, I looked around for my walker. In the confusion, someone had moved it—I didn't see it anywhere. Before I panicked, I noticed someone's wheelchair staring at me. Without wasting a moment, I grabbed it, hopped in, and headed for the door.

This seemingly endless ordeal had only taken a few minutes. Out on the lawn, a crowd of about 500 people stood, waiting for some word on what was going on. At that point, we learned that it had been only a drill. To make it seem real, not even the therapists had been told in advance. The hospital staff wanted to see how everyone would react. Things hadn't gone very smoothly, at least in the physical therapy room. One thing was certain, though. They'd scared the devil out of me!

That night a fellow insurance salesman and friend of mine, Karl Steen, called to say he and his wife would be by tomorrow for a visit. This was exciting. It would be their second time at Woodrow, and I wanted to show them how much I'd improved. Their first visit had been shortly after my admittance, when I couldn't do much of anything for myself. I had a few surprises in mind for them.

Shortly after lunch the next day, Karl and Liz arrived. I was sitting in my wheelchair when they walked into the room. When I stood up and gave Liz a hug, she almost passed out. Then a big smile came over her face.

"I can't believe it!" she exclaimed.

We went to the Recreation Center, where it was quieter, and had a nice visit. I told them about the skills I'd attained in occupational therapy and how much less I had to depend on my wheelchair for mobility. Chatting with them about my progress made me realize that maybe I really was ready to go home.

The reason we needed to go some place quierter was because of my new roommate. Although I went out of my way to get along with him, it was useless. He was self-centered, thinking only of himself. Unfortunately, he was on the same side of the room as I was, which meant that we shared a television set. In the past, I'd taken turns with my roommates so that each of us got a chance to watch a fair share of our favorite shows. This man wanted his own way 100 percent of the time.

His reaction when he didn't get his way was worse than his attitude. The language he used would make the Devil cringe— it's a wonder they didn't terminate him. I'm sure that everyone who'd come in contact with him would have jumped for joy. If I tried to watch a program, he would play his radio full blast. His favorite type of music was hard rock. Simply put, he was driving me nuts. And the noise continued until 11:00 P.M., when everyone had to turn off all televisions and radios.

All day Saturday, we'd gone through this routine, and by 11:00, I was a nervous wreck. My head was pounding. At least now it'll be quiet, I thought to myself as I closed my eyes.

Then I heard a noise that sounded like a motor running. I rang my bell for the nurses and asked someone to come in and find out what the problem was. It was my roommate again. He was sitting there with his hair dryer blowing on him. He claimed that he was sweaty, and this was the only way he could dry the perspiration on his body. Would you believe that the nurse let him keep that thing going *all night*? I just couldn't sleep under those conditions. It wasn't just the noise, either. I kept thinking about what a fire hazard it was—what if the motor overheated and caught the bed on fire? Maybe I was paranoid after my scare in physical therapy during the fire drill, but to me it was a real threat.

On Sunday things got worse. He was up at 7:30 and going at it again. I'd had about all I could stand. As soon as I got dressed, I put a John Denver tape in my cassette player—he hated John Denver—and turned up the volume as loud as it would go. Then I left the room. The noise was deafening. I must admit, I did it just to be spiteful, and I felt a bit ashamed of myself. But everyone's got a breaking point.

When I returned to my room, there stood a nurse and one of the hospital administrators. We had a long talk, and they told me they fully understood my frustration. But no one else would room with him.

"We thought maybe being around you might make a difference in him," the administrator said. "But I guess we were wrong."

We all discussed the problem with my roommate, and the two of us agreed to turn down our volume knobs. The minute they left though, his was turned up again. By evening I was shorting out like a frayed wire. Something had to be done.

The first thing Monday morning, I went to see Duane for help. Right away, he called the nurses station to see about transferring me to another room. He was told that they would try, but it might take four or five days to work things out. I begged Duane to see if something could be done sooner than that. My nerves weren't going to hold out much longer. He promised to do what he could.

When I returned from therapy that afternoon, Savoy and Bobby, two aides, were in my room piling all of my things onto the bed.

"We have orders to move you to another room," explained Savoy. "As soon as you return from supper, we should have all of your things out of the drawers and closets and ready to roll."

"Let's do it right now," I said. "I'll order something to eat from the cafeteria later tonight." But they had to help with supper, so I would have to wait.

As soon as I had finished eating, I went back to my room. Savoy and Bobby came in soon thereafter.

"Let's get this show on the road," said Bobby. I was ready, and we proceeded down the hall to the new room. It turned out to be a two-bed room like Terry and Kenny's. I thought they had the only one in the unit. What a pleasant surprise after such a hassle, I thought.

My new roommate was Billy White, a young man who'd been in a car accident and had suffered extensive brain damage. He was blind and almost totally paralyzed. He was also unable to speak.

Once again I was struck by how fortunate I was. There were a lot of people who were much worse off than I was, and because of the extent of their injuries, they might stay that way—permanently.

For the remainder of my stay at Woodrow, I remained in this room. I thoroughly enjoyed the peace and quiet. I came and went whenever I pleased and watched television whenever I wished. I tried asking Billy if there was anything he'd like to listen to, but he couldn't understand me.

Until my accident, I had never realized the amount of human suffering and misery we have here in the United States. Sure, I'd traveled all over the world. I'd seen misery and poverty. But that was material deprivation and seemed far removed from the real world that I knew in America.

Here was all this mental and physical misery, right on my doorstep, and I'd never seen it. How I wished I had a magic wand to wave over all these wretched bodies and minds, transforming them back into vital, whole human beings.

That night I had difficulty sleeping again. This time it wasn't noise from the outside of my body; it was noise from within. People say that everything that happens has a purpose in God's overall plan. What was this plan, I wanted to know. Why does something like this have to be? The things I had seen and experienced certainly tested my faith. But I tenaciously hung on to my belief in Him. Even if I didn't understand what the plan was, it was there—it had to be.

By Friday, October 16, I could walk to therapy and back to my room without the aid of a walker. The first few times that I tried walking on my own, I stayed close to the wall. When I stumbled, which was often, I could fall against the wall and catch myself. But the more practice I got, the farther away from supports, like the wall, I could get without the fear of crashing down onto the floor. The exertion and concentration it took to walk were draining. No wonder babies hold onto the edge of the coffee table for so long—and they've got the advantage of being closer to the ground. Relearning how to walk was taking more time and effort than I could ever have imagined. I had done it, though. Of course, I had a lot more work to do to improve, but considering how many people thought I could *never* do it, I was making excellent progress. Another goal was accomplished—it was not finished, it might never be finished, I might never have the natural, flowing gait of my preaccident self—yet there was no denying the fact that I really could walk.

I was improving in other areas as well. My right hand could now function at about 70 percent of its former capacity, although my left hand was still almost useless. Thank goodness I was right-handed.

There was no longer a bowel program to endure. I had regained normal bowel function and was eating regular meals. You can't imagine how thrilled I was to learn that I wouldn't have to put up with the embarrassment of this miserable daily ritual at home.

Sitting in my wheelchair and supporting my elbow on the table at the sink, I could shave, wash my face, put on deodorant, and brush my teeth. I still couldn't comb my hair because I couldn't reach up high enough or get to the back of my head.

I could dress myself now, but some of the tasks were more difficult than others. Getting my shirt on was tough. I couldn't raise my arms more than 20°, so putting both arms in the sleeves and hiking the shirt up over my shoulders was a real challenge. And then there were the buttons. It took awhile to do, but I managed to get the job done. Tying my shoes was not so easy, either.

Sometimes I'd get very frustrated with myself for not being able to do some of these things as quickly or as well as I would've liked. I had to constantly remind myself that these were skills that took most children the first five or six years of their lives to learn. Although my mind remembered how to do these jobs, my muscles had to learn them from scratch. "It's a cinch by the inch, but hard by the yard" was so true. And my inches were beginning to add up.

As the time for my discharge approached, many students told me how much they'd miss me. They looked up to me, almost worshipped me as someone who had attempted the impossible and succeeded. I began spending most of my spare time talking with them, trying to help them see the positive side of life. I wasn't out to paint rosy pictures for them or give them false hope. By my example, I wanted to show them what they could accomplish if they were willing to pay the price—spiritually and mentally, as well as physically.

On Monday morning, one of the students gave me one of the most soul-satisfying experiences of my life. I was sitting on a bench in physical therapy when I spotted Tommy Elridge, a former roommate of mine from the University of Virginia hospital. Tommy was up and walking with leg braces and crutches. He slowly hobbled over and sat down beside me.

"I want to thank you, Morris," he said.

"For what?" I asked.

"For giving me the courage to walk," Tommy replied. "Back when we were both in the University Hospital and I was really suffering and feeling sorry for myself, your courage came shining through. I would lie in bed and look at you, with all your problems, and you were always smiling and giving encouragement to everyone. Then I would start to feel ashamed of myself.

"My problems, bad as they were, were nothing compared to yours. It took several months for it to really sink in, though. You don't know it, but one day not long ago, I was here in therapy when you were struggling to learn to walk. I watched as you stumbled and fell, picked yourself back up, and kept going. That day I said to myself, if he can do it with all he's been through, then so can I.

"A hundred therapists and doctors can tell a person the same thing, but seeing it for yourself is the greatest convincer in the world. That day, I made a commitment to myself to get out of my wheelchair. So I just want to say thanks."

Well, for the rest of the day, I don't think my feet touched the ground. I felt so fulfilled, knowing that I had helped someone else gain the courage and determination to fight life's battles on his own. Zig Ziglar's famous line, "You can get everything in life that you want if you will just help enough other people get what they want," came to mind. I had helped Tommy, and he had helped me. This is what makes life worth living.

On Wednesday night, while I was watching television, a nurse named Betty Galope came in carrying what looked like a guitar case. Sure enough, that's what it was.

"I brought something for you," she said. "This guitar was sitting around my house collecting dust, and I thought you might enjoy playing it while you were here." Before I could say anything, she put it down and walked out.

She must be crazy, I said to myself. Me play a guitar? Why, that's ridiculous. Before my accident, I had been an accomplished guitarist, and I truly missed playing. But with my crippled hands, there was no way I could play. The temptation to try was just too great, though.

I slowly hobbled out of my wheelchair and over to the case. With persistence, I managed to get the guitar case open and lift out the guitar. Lacking the strength to hold it, I sat on the bed with it across my lap. Then I tried to play the simple cord of D. For 30 minutes I struggled, but to no avail.

With a smile on my face, I got the guitar back in its case. This was a new challenge. If it takes me 20 years, I told myself, I will play again.

The next afternoon, Thursday, October 22, I was in physical therapy watching a group that had gathered around Frankie Campbell and one of the therapists. Frankie still asked people how they were doing, but not as frequently nor as many times in a row. We could carry on a limited conversation, and his short-term memory was improving, though his long-term memory was still rather vague.

I got up and walked over to where everyone was gathered. Franklie look at me with a distant expression.

"Hey, buddy, how are you doing?" he asked.

"Just fine, Frankie," I answered.

"Don't I know you from somewhere?" he continued. "What is your name?"

"Ronald Reagan," I replied.

"Ronald Reagan, are you really Ronald Reagan?" he asked.

"Why, I voted for you," said Frankie as he reached out to shake my hand. "Where are you from?"

"Dover Hollow," I said without hesitation.

"Dover Hollow!" he exclaimed. "Why, that's where I'm

from. I've never seen you there before." By now, chuckles were coming from the group. "Who is your father?" Frankie asked next.

"Archie Campbell," I said.

"Archie Campbell," he mused with glazed eyes. "Why, he's my father, too. I guess we must be sisters."

At this, everyone burst out laughing. We weren't trying to make fun of Frankie or be cruel. Frankie enjoyed the attention, and we all enjoyed the best medicine in the world—laughter. Unfortunately, about a week later, Frankie was sent home. They said that when he showed some improvement, he could return for treatment. I don't know what he's doing today, but I hope Frankie is doing okay. He gave many of us at Woodrow a chance to lighten up, to smile, when it seemed as if there wasn't anything in the world to be happy about. Thanks again, Frankie.

For several months, I'd been concerned about falling, especially now that I was getting around by myself. If I ended on the floor, that's where I stayed until someone came by to pick me up. I just didn't have enough strength in my legs and enough balance to get up on my own. At Woodrow, this wasn't really a problem since someone was always watching out for me. The staff told me not to worry about this limitation, but I did worry.

At home it would be a horse of a different color. Naturally, if there was someone there, I could get help. But I didn't want to have to depend on someone having to be there all the time. It would be too much of a burden—on myself and on others. So I had set a goal for myself. Before I was discharged, I would be able to get up off the ground without any help.

I'd been working on this for the last several weeks. Each day, I spent several hours strengthening my legs and working on my balance using the parallel bars. Whenever one of the therapists was free, I would lie on the floor and try to get up. I'd usually make it about halfway up, but then my legs would give way, I'd lose my balance, and the therapist would catch me to break my fall.

On Friday, October 23—just three weeks before my discharge date—I had a gut feeling that this would be the day I'd make it all the way up on my feet. After doing some light exercises so that I wouldn't wear out my legs, I sat and rested for almost an hour. I kept visualizing myself getting up off the floor without any help. Once I felt psyched up and ready to go, I asked Dave if he would guard me. I got down on the floor. Here goes, I thought. I was almost all the way up when I lost it and fell back.

"You want to try again?" Dave asked.

"You bet I do," I replied. I closed my eyes and concentrated as hard as I could. I started; kept going; kept going—and made it!

"Let's try again," I said. Once more, I made it all the way up, all by myself. Look out world, here I come, I thought. Nothing can stop me now. I had succeeded again, was one more step closer to full recovery, through sheer determination and willpower. The positive, can-do attitude that had made me a success in sales was going to make me successful at living a normal life again.

That weekend, I spent most of my time listening to my collection of motivational tapes. Three of my closest friends—Terry, Kenny, and John—had been discharged. John Marshall, another close friend, was due for discharge early the coming week. In three more weeks, it would be my turn. It was time to recharge my batteries and get ready for this last big push at recovery. Sure, I'd continue to work on my skills at home, but I needed to learn as many techniques as I could so that I could better direct myself. Going home wasn't an inch to be cinched, it wasn't even a yard—it was going to feel like miles, and I had to be prepared.

For the past ten years, I'd accumulated quite a collection of books and tapes on motivation. They numbered in the hundreds and were by such noted authors as Dr. Robert Schuller, Dr. Norman Vincent Peale, Earl Nightingale, Og Mandino, W. Clement Stone, Napoleon Hill, and Cavett Roberts.

One set of tapes kept me coming back over and over again. I never got tired of listening to them; in fact, I still listen to them today. They are by the master of motivational speaking, Zig Ziglar. His enthusiasm and his ability to communicate can be matched by none. His book *See You at the Top* is a classic. I advise anyone who is looking for direction in this complex world of ours to invest in some books and tapes by Zig or by any of the other fine motivational authors. Once you do, you'll be hooked for good.

By the time I closed my eyes Sunday night, I felt like a new man. My batteries were fully charged, and I was ready to go out and fight tigers, or at least those uncooperative muscles that I needed to whip back into shape.

I realized that returning to the outside world would be like being born again. My umbilical cord would be cut, severing me from the shelter and protection of the womb—Woodrow. The world would be a much colder and more hostile environment. Adjustment would be up to me, not to others. In order to fit back into the slot I'd vacated, I'd have to put forth an enormous amount of effort.

To make the transition easier, I hoped to equip my house with some of the exercise machines I used daily. These would continue to help me improve my muscle tone. On Monday night, October 26, I called my good friends, Bill Hermann and Page Scott, to ask a favor. Both are very skilled with their hands, and I hoped that they would be able to re-create some of the equipment I needed.

Two machines were high on my priority list. One was the sander—the box in which weights were placed to improve upper body strength. The other was a cylinder-shaped machine with a handle extending from it. I referred to this as a wrist machine because it helped increase the range of motion in my wrists and forearms. Weights could be added to give more resistance. I had full supination, or flexibility, in my right hand, but could barely turn the machine with my left. Because both of these machines were built by the engineering department at Woodrow, you couldn't buy them from a store or a catalog. Bill's and Page's skill and creativity were just what I needed.

They agreed to come up, look at the machines, make some sketches, and see about building something similar for me. On Tuesday morning, Page called and said he and Bill planned to fly up on Wednesday morning.

"I'll fly to Norfolk and pick up Bill. We should be there before 11:00," Page informed me.

"I'll be waiting for you," I told him. When the chips were down, I could really depend on those guys.

Bill and Page arrived at 10:45 A.M. on Wednesday. They were really happy to see me, and the feeling was mutual. We chatted about their flight. As they described the fine weather and the beautiful fall scenery, I wished that I could have been with them. We headed for the occupational therapy room. After

I had introduced them to some of the therapists and explained what we wanted to do, Bill and Page got to work—Bill making sketches and Page taking measurements.

"This won't be any problem at all," Page said. "I can make that wrist machine without any trouble." Then Bill assured me that he could take care of the sander.

It was almost time for lunch, so I asked them to stay and go to the cafeteria with me. I hadn't eaten there for quite a while. Usually I went to the dining room so that I could get help with my food and not have so far to travel. As we headed for the door, Duane appeared.

"I want to introduce you to a couple of friends of mine," I said. I made the introductions, and when Duane was ready to leave, he looked at me and shook his head.

"I really fooled you, didn't I?" I said.

"You sure did," he replied. "When you first came here, I wouldn't have given a plug nickel for you."

"Now he's worth at least a quarter," Page added. Duane just smiled and walked on.

After lunch I walked with Bill and Page back to the administration building to wait for their cab. When it was time for them to leave, I realized that this time it wouldn't be months before I saw my friends again. I'd be home soon.

"I'll see you in a few weeks," I said as they got into the cab. My discharge date was rapidly approaching. The impossible was finally going to happen.

The recreation department had planned an outing for Thursday night. The trip was to a nearby town for dinner at a restaurant. We all would be responsible for our own bills, but Woodrow was supplying the transportation as well as several people to help the students with wheelchairs and with their feeding. It sounded like a good chance to get out with the gang for one last hurrah.

Around 5:00 that evening, about 20 of us gathered in the administration building to wait for the bus. Soon our transportation arrived, and I was disturbed to find that it was the same bus that had thrown me several months ago when I was returning to The Towers from my tour of Woodrow. I'd sworn that I wouldn't tempt fate again by riding in it, but I relented and climbed aboard. Of course, we made it into town without any problems, but the trip was certainly not relaxing for me, and I breathed an audible sigh of relief when I was back on solid, stationary ground again.

Crab cakes were on the menu, and I couldn't resist. I was aching for some real seafood as a reminder of home and a treat to my tastebuds. But I should have waited until I could go to a restaurant a little closer to the ocean. Fresh seafood is tremendous. Seafood in the mountains is just food. I was letting my expectations run away with me again. The meal was edible; it just wasn't what I'd wished for.

Nevertheless, the evening was pleasant. The joy of getting out for the night with some friends and sharing a few laughs was well worth the tension of the trip and the minor disappointment of dinner. For several hours, we all forgot about our troubles and enjoyed ourselves.

Friday afternoon, October 30, marked the end of another week. My discharge date was only two weeks away. Now that I was used to the idea, I was counting down the days with enthusiasm instead of anxiety.

After I had finished therapy that day, I bumped into Duane.

"Got a minute?" he asked.

"Sure," I replied.

"Meet me in my office. I'd like to talk with you for just a minute," he told me. So I continued down the hall and waited for him. About five minutes later, he came in, closed the door, and sat down across from me.

"Well, how do you feel about leaving?" he asked.

"I feel pretty comfortable now," I answered. "Before, I was worried, but not any longer."

We continued to chat about my upcoming big move. Then Duane looked at me. His expression was quite serious, and I hoped he didn't have something discouraging to say.

"You know," he began, "I learn something from everyone I work with."

"What have you learned from me?" I asked.

"You know," Duane continued, "all my life I've studied positive mental attitude. I've read books, listened to tapes, gone to seminars. And I thought I understood what it was all about. That is, until you came along. For the first time, I saw someone take it and make it work. I've learned the real meaning of positive mental attitude from you. Your short stay here will leave a lasting impression on me."

I was stepping pretty high when I left his office that afternoon. Here was someone who had had years of training in
counseling and had dealt with hundreds of students a year.
Yet he'd learned something valuable from me. He'd seen that
positive thinking can do more than change someone's attitude
from bad to good. It can change a life. Instead of smiling con-
tentedly from my wheelchair, I had used the positive power of
self-confidence to push myself to the limit, to improve myself
as much as I possibly could. And I wasn't finished yet, either.

Just when I felt that I was ready for my freedom and had
accepted the adjustments I would have to make, I once again
experienced mixed emotions. The time for my discharge was
approaching like a runaway locomotive coming straight at me,
and I was powerless to get out of its way. The world I'd known
for 35 years was going to seem mighty foreign to me. Going
home was necessary, it was what I wanted, it was what I'd
been shooting for, but it wasn't going to be easy.

I had a couple of surprise visits during my last two weeks
at Woodrow. One night, during the first week of November, I
was sitting in my room waiting for a pizza to arrive by cab.
Because the hospital menu hadn't been too appealing, I'd decided to treat myself. Since Terry and Kenny had left, I'd almost
stopped sending out for pizza. But tonight, I planned on having
a lonely, though delicious, meal.

When I heard someone come through the door, I turned
my wheelchair around, expecting to see the cab driver. There
stood my friend and attorney, Mel Friedman, and his fiance,
Phyllis. Mel explained that they were on a camping trip and
had decided to stop by. I talked them into sharing my pizza
with me, and we had a nice visit.

As they were leaving, I told them I'd see them in a few
weeks. Mel knew about my discharge date, but Phyllis seemed
surprised.

"We'll have to get together for a cookout," she said.

"You bet," I replied. "I'll be looking forward to it!"

The thought of not having any visitors really bothered me
on one particular day—Monday, November 9. It was my birthday. I really missed getting together with my family for cake
and ice cream, singing "Happy Birthday," and opening my
presents. I guess I'm still a little kid at heart.

This birthday was going to be a sad occasion. As far as I

could remember, this would be the first time that I'd celebrated it alone. When I returned to my room after therapy that afternoon, there was a package on my bed. I immediately rounded up a nurse to open it for me.

Sandy had timed the arrival of my present perfectly. She'd picked out a beautiful pair of pants and a matching sweater, and, of course, there was a card. Sandy picks out the most wonderful cards and then adds her own thoughts and love at the bottom. Her gift and card made up for some of the emptiness, but it just wasn't the same.

As soon as I had finished supper, she called to wish me a happy birthday. Then my mother, sister, and Sandy's parents called. Speaking to everyone really cheered me up. The day was almost over. Maybe I'd just turn in early.

As I was walking back to my room from the telephone, one of the nurses approached me.

"There's someone to see you in the dining room," she said. I couldn't imagine who it could be.

"Happy birthday!" shouted everyone as I entered the room. There stood about 20 friends, complete with cake and ice cream. I blew out the candles, and we all dug in. What a fine birthday after all, I said to myself that night. And just four more days until I'm home at last.

On Thursday evening, I spoke with Sandy to make sure all bases had been covered. The transition would be smoother if we made sure there weren't things we'd forgotten. She and Pat planned on arriving around 10:00 the next day. My discharge hearing was set for 11:00. If all went well, we'd be on the road by noon.

Discharge day. Friday the Thirteenth. It sounded rather ominous, but I've never been superstitious. I was up and dressed bright and early, and one of the nurses helped me pack. Once everything was boxed and ready to go, I was amazed at how much there was. Sandy and Pat found me pacing nervously when they came in, right on time. They started packing the car immediately so that we could leave as soon as the meeting was over.

About 20 minutes before the meeting was due to begin, I handed out some gifts to the staff and said my goodbyes. I'd asked Sandy and Pat to pick up a few things for the people who'd worked with me. They'd bought some beautifully framed and matted prints of Norfolk, Virginia, as it had been 50 to 100 years ago. All of them were painted by a talented historical artist, Casey Holtzinger.

In physical therapy, mat class was in progress. I stood there watching for a minute or two; then Martha stopped the class, and everyone shouted a hearty send-off to me. It was the only time since I'd been there that I'd seen mat class come to a halt. As I turned and walked away, I could hear their counting in time with Martha. They were back to business as usual.

Finally it was time for my discharge meeting to begin. Sandy, Pat, and I headed for the conference room, where I'd spent my last moments at Woodrow Wilson.

Two of the people who should have been there couldn't make it. A counselor by the name of Becky Messer sat in for Duane Anderson. And Irene McClay, a physical therapist, sat in for my regular physical therapist, Dave Summer. Neither of the substitutes had worked with me or knew about my case personally. There were some familiar faces, though. Betty, from nursing; Meg, from occupational therapy; and Dr. Richard M. Auld, who'd taken over Dr. Spicuzza's role as the doctor in charge of my case, were all in attendance.

Meg led off. She summarized my accomplishments in occupational therapy and ended by saying that she felt I could use some more work on fine motor skills. Next Betty said that, in her opinion, I needed very little help in self-care and personal hygiene.

Then it was Becky's turn. She recommended that I get further counseling to learn to cope with my handicap. How in the world could she make a statement like that? She doesn't even know me, I thought to myself. I almost said something but decided to bite my tongue. No need to create waves now. In a few minutes, it will all be over, and I'll be gone for good.

As soon as Becky had finished, Irene chimed in. She recommended that I go home and learn to live with things as they were. She felt that further physical therapy would be useless. I could have screamed, but I kept quiet. This whole meeting is becoming ridiculous, I thought to myself. I was also thinking about my insurance. Unless my discharge papers stated that I required further treatment, my policy would not cover the expenses of therapy sessions once I was home. I knew that I needed more help.

At last, it was Dr. Auld's turn. He was more realistic. He believed that further extensive physical therapy would be needed, and this is what he indicated in the discharge summary he'd prepared. That ended the meeting. All the people at the meeting wished me the best and asked me to stay in touch and let them know how I was progressing.

The noonday sun flooded my senses and warmed the brisk, late autumn air as we pulled away from the place that had served as my home for five long months. An indescribable joy and elation filled me with hope for the future. My journey home had been a hard and grueling one. But I'd persevered and succeeded, overcoming incredible odds, the never-ending doubts of those around me, and muscles that I had not let rest until they performed the duties forgotten after the trauma of my accident and weeks of uselessness. As Zig Ziglar says, "I had not paid the price for victory. I was enjoying the price."

chapter **10**

A NEW BEGINNING

But what if I fail of my purpose here?
It is but to keep the nerves at strain,
To dry one's eyes and laugh at a fall,
And, baffled, get up and begin again.

ELIZABETH BARRETT BROWNING

Just as everything had been routine, the same, day after day while I was hospitalized and in rehabilitation, now they were different, new, a gauntlet thrown down to challenge my adaptability. The house; relationships with my family and friends; therapists; pain-relief techniques—everything and everyone represented a change.

First, there was the house. Sandy and I could not afford to maintain the high standard of living we'd enjoyed before my crash. So we had decided on a modest townhouse in place of our former palacial home. The day of my discharge, Sandy was bubbling over with enthusiasm, eager to show me what she had done to the new place. She had used some of our furniture from the previous house and made the place look really nice. Everything was unboxed and arranged neatly. How she had managed to do it all in less than two weeks with no help was beyond me. Still, it would take me some time to adjust to the new rooms, the new neighborhood, my new home.

One especially challenging aspect of the house was the staircase. We'd installed an extra handrail so that there was one on each side of the steps, but getting up and down 14 stairs was not easy. The bedrooms were upstairs, and I was always thankful to have something cozy to rest on once I'd made it to the top. Coming down was a different story—it meant the beginning of a long day of pain and exercise. But the practice was necessary for improving my leg muscles and balance, since I would have to go up and down stairs somewhere, anyway.

Although my family and friends were extremely supportive, our relationships had changed because of the accident. I was no longer a completely independent human being. Despite my enormous efforts, I was going to need assistance with simple things like combing my hair as well as more time-consuming activities such as transporting me to my therapy sessions. My progress since the crash had been phenomenal, but I was far from being the fast-track salesman of my former days, flying here and there for meetings and speeches. I had limits. I had made it a point to constantly stretch those limits. But they were still there.

I would have a new set of therapists. This meant getting to know each other, testing my abilities, deciding on a program—all these in addition to the basic tasks of finding them and getting to their offices for appointments.

Physical and occupational therapy could help me improve my muscle coordination and skills, but they wouldn't help alleviate the intense burning sensations that continued to plague me. Surely there must be some way to rid myself of the pain, I thought. I was determined to try any techniques that could possibly lessen if not eliminate this torture.

Yes, I had quite a bit of adjusting to do, and I had a lot of work ahead of me before I could say I was fully recovered. But, for the first time in eight months, I could adjust and work and relax in a place I called home.

I spent the first week and a half at home resting and getting used to my new surroundings and routines. Before I knew it, it was Thanksgiving. When I'd been at The Towers, I'd sworn I'd never eat turkey again but now I dug into that holiday bird like a starving man. Mother had us over for the day, and she had prepared a feast fit for a king. The company was grand, too. My aunts, Hilda, Dorothy, and Eloise, were there. Pat and her daughter, Ashley, came. I even had a visit from my cousin, Ted, when he stopped in later in the day. It turned out to be the best Thanksgiving I'd ever had.

On Monday morning, November 30, rest time was over. I decided that it was time to get down to business. So I started my search for both a physical and an occupational therapist. After numerous calls and inquiries, I discovered a physical therapist named Diane Petry, who lived within a few miles of my house, and who had her own facilities. I set up an appointment so that we could meet, talk about my condition, and see if she felt that she could help me.

A few days later, when I arrived at her office, I was surprised to see an old friend, Garrett Snyder. Garrett had worked at Woodrow Wilson, doing his final affiliation, when I was there, and he'd worked with me, so he was familiar with my condition.

"What are you doing here?" I asked.

"Just filling in for a few weeks," he replied. "Have a seat for a minute, and I'll show you around."

When Garrett returned, I got a tour of the place. The facilities were small but adequate, and I couldn't beat the location, since it was so close to home. Then I talked with Diane. She assured me that she could help me improve my balance and walking skills, so we set up an appointment for evaluation.

"I understand you're looking for an occupational therapist," Diane commented.

"I sure am," I replied.

She told me that she knew of an excellent therapist. That's great, I thought. For once, things were easier than I'd expected—two therapists at one shot. Diane said she'd contact the therapist and ask her to get in touch with me.

That night a woman by the name of Susan Morales called. She said that her specialty was hand therapy. Could she come out and see me? I almost jumped through the phone saying yes. That's exactly what I needed. So I set up an appointment for her to come to the house. Now things were really moving along.

But I still had to do something about the pain in the lower half of my body. The burning sensation was becoming unbearable. All day, and worse at night, regardless of my position or how often I changed it, the pain continued. There was no relief. You know what it's like when you burn your finger. That one tiny area of pain can drive you crazy. Imagine half of your body feeling like that—all of the time.

The doctors attributed this pain to nerve damage resulting from my spinal cord injury. Some people with these injuries feel this pain even if they have no other feeling or sensations because of paralysis. Sometimes it gets better. Sometimes it goes away. Sometimes it doesn't. I wasn't just going to wait around and see what happened.

I'd spoken with Duane Anderson about this problem and had also told him about the constant ache in my neck and shoulders. A television program about the ancient Chinese art of acupuncture had captured my attention, and I hoped he could suggest someone to see. At the time, Duane said he knew of no one in the area who practiced acupuncture. But he did say that he's seen some favorable results at another rehabilitation center. So a specialist in acupuncture was next on my therapy shopping list. Surely, in an area as big as Tidewater, there had to be someone.

After asking friends, family, and medical people, I finally got the name of Dr. Robert K. Su from a cousin of mine. His office, located in Portsmouth, Virginia, would be an hour's drive away, but it was worth a try. I called his nurse and begged for an appointment. At first, she tried to put me off for three weeks, but I pleaded my case, and she agreed to work me in the next day.

When I saw Dr. Su the following day, I was impressed with his straightforward attitude. He made no false promises, nor did he paint a dismal picture of my condition.

"I have never seen an injury such as yours," he explained. "I cannot promise you anything, but I am willing to give it a try." Well, that was good enough for me. He would need a full medical report from Dr. Rish before he could begin treatment, so I would have another wait.

"I'll give him a call tomorrow and plan on seeing you back here in two weeks," Dr. Su said. As much as I hated the delay, there was nothing I could do about it. I'd suffered for almost nine months. A couple more weeks wouldn't kill me.

One week before Christmas, Friday, December 18, the Norfolk Life Underwriters Association was having its end-of-the-year meeting. For as long as I could remember, they'd had this meeting just before Christmas—it was a tradition. I'd been a part of the association, made up of over 500 life insurance agents from the Norfolk area, since I first entered the business in 1971. But I wasn't just a member. I'd taken an active role, serving on many committees as well as on the board of directors. The members were my friends. Although we were in a competitive business, we shared our lives, our friendship, and our love.

The common goals we shared that kept us going were these: to make the world a better place to live and to ease the financial hardship caused by the death of a family's breadwinner. The ability to care about others really came out when everyone learned of my accident. Cards and letters had poured in by the hundreds. One agent with Minnesota Mutual, Russ Gills, had offered to help run my business until I got back on my feet. I had cried like a baby when the nurse read his letter to me.

So that Friday morning, more than anything else on earth, I wanted to attend that meeting. I wanted to feel as though I really belonged again. Luckily, a neighbor and longtime friend, Jim Parker, offered to take me. He is an agent with Jefferson Standard and is a member himself.

Everyone was surprised to see me. Phil Todd, the president, insisted that Jim and I sit at the head table. After opening the meeting, Phil began commenting on my return. You could have heard a pin drop—it was intensely quiet. His speech was brief, yet touching. He concluded by saying, "I think Winston Churchill put it best when he said, 'Never give in, never, never, never, never.' "

With a thunderous roar, they all rose to their feet and applauded. There wasn't a dry eye in the house. What a special moment this was—one that I will never, ever forget.

By Christmas I'd settled into a rigorous schedule that barely gave me time to breathe and eat. Now that I was home, I could clearly see my limitations. Like a driven man, I felt that I could not rest until I'd accomplished as much as was humanly possible. My desire for a normal life challenged me at every turn. I wanted to walk without fear of stumbling. I wanted to drive a car, I wanted to improve my eye-hand coordination and increase my strength enough to hunt again. I was determined to meet these challenges.

On Monday, Wednesday, and Friday, I would dress, eat breakfast, and arrive at Diane's office for a 9:00 to 10:30 session of physical therapy. Then I would go home to eat lunch and rest my neck for a few minutes. At 1:30 Sandy and I would leave for Dr. Su's office in Portsmouth. We usually didn't leave his office until 4:30. Because of the hour of driving and the time it took for the doctor to see me and finish my treatment, it was 6:30 or 7:00 P.M. by the time we got home and had dinner.

On Tuesday, Thursday, and Saturday, the morning began with a visit by Susan, my occupational therapist. Then, after lunch, I'd work out in my home gym for about four hours.

Sunday was the only day I allowed myself to rest. Often,

we went to visit my mother on my day off. The first few weeks of this hectic schedule went very well. But soon Sandy began feeling the strain of so much traveling. Because I couldn't drive, she had to provide all my transportation, and it was wearing her out. For the time being, though, we agreed that taking a chance on the acupuncture treatments was necessary. Until I was certain that they weren't helping me, or until I had an alternative, I needed to do *something* about the pain, for psychological as well as physical reasons.

Christmas gave both of us a welcome break. Susan and Dr. Su were going out of town and weren't due to return until after New Year's. So I canceled my physical therapy sessions until then. This gave us a week and a half of rest, rest that we both desperately needed.

Christmas Day was a happy family occasion. We all gathered at my mother's house to celebrate our being together for another year. Pat and Ashley were there, as well as two of my aunts. After exchanging gifts, we all settled down to a delicious dinner. I was still getting enormous pleasure out of good home cooking after so many months of institutional food. Before eating, we said a special blessing and thanked God for allowing me to be there on this joyous day.

The sun was setting as Sandy and I pulled into our driveway that day. I was so exhausted that I would have sworn it was midnight, if the richly colored hues of dusk hadn't told me otherwise. My clothes were off and my pajamas were on in no time at all. Just as I was preparing to settle in for a nap, the doorbell rang. Who in the world can that be, I wondered. I hitched up my bathrobe over my shoulders and made my way downstairs to answer the door. There stood Dr. Oden's daughter, Cathy.

She told me that she could only stay a minute and didn't want to interrupt my rest, but her father had wanted me to have his Christmas gift today. Then she handed me the large cardboard box she was holding. Soon she was gone, and I asked Sandy to open the box. The suspense was killing me. Inside the package were the most beautiful oranges I'd ever seen. Leonard had ordered them from Florida, so I was sure that they were as fresh and delicious as they looked. We weren't disappointed. Sandy and I had a grand time devouring a much appreciated treat. As soon as I finished licking the juice from my fingers and got back upstairs, I called Leonard and his wife, Ginny, to thank them.

"We'll see you on Sunday," Leonard chuckled, clearly enjoying my pleasure over his gift.

Leonard did come on Sunday, and so did many others. They all helped me celebrate my victory over the odds. Back in March, no one would have believed I would be home for Christmas, let alone in my present condition. Back in March, everyone had thought they'd seen the last of poor old Morris. But I'm a survivor, a winner, a salesman who sold himself on life. With willpower, mindpower, and the power of Almighty God, I'd beaten all the odds. I guess He wasn't finished with me yet. Despite the pain and my handicaps, that was fine with me.

On Thursday night, December 31, as the final seconds of 1981 ticked away, I prayed that none of us would ever have to live through another year as traumatic as this one. My accident had altered many people's lives. Those closest to me were acutely affected emotionally and financially. Even friends and acquaintances had been touched, as if my plane had been a pebble dropped into a pond sending out ripples that dissipate slowly, losing their force as they reach out over an increasingly wide and distant surface. I hoped that no more pebbles would be dropped, that our lives would continue now, calmly and smoothly, like an undisturbed pond.

That weekend I took stock of my situation. The holidays were over, and it was time to attack my therapy programs with a vengeance. There were so many areas that needed to be worked on that I decided to list my top priorities. This would give me specific tasks to focus on and would break down the overwhelming job of recovery into smaller, more manageable steps.

The most compelling problem was the constant burning and pain I felt in my lower body. At times it was so bad that I wanted to pound my head against the wall. Somewhere there had to be an answer. If the acupuncture didn't work, I would find some other type of therapy.

Another pressing concern was the lack of strength in my shoulders. My deltoids, the muscles covering the shoulder blades, and shoulder girdle, which normally supports the arms, were atrophied. They were so weak that I could only raise my arms about 20° (all the way over my head would be 180°, so I had a long way to go). This meant that I couldn't put on a pullover shirt, handle a heavy coat, or get a glass down from the cabinet. I shaved and ate by supporting my elbow on the table. Back at Woodrow, the therapists had said I would never regain the ability to raise my arms over my head. I had other plans.

Of course, no amount of strength in my arms and shoulders could compensate for normal hand function. Susan was confident that we could get my hands back into a working state with practice. And boy, did I practice! She gave me all sorts of exercises to do using clay, rubber bands, clothespins, pegs, and custom-made equipment. I was sure that if I kept working on them, they'd continue to improve. When I wasn't using them, my fingers were kept open by using hand splints Susan had made. Just like the toes on my left foot, my hands tended to rest in a clenched position and were difficult to release. The splints made doing everything else harder, though.

My legs also needed strengthening. I could walk only about 100 steps before they began to buckle and refused to support me. Here again, the muscles had gotten out of practice and had to be retrained.

But this wasn't the only problem I had with walking. My balance was so poor that every two or three steps I took, I'd start to fall and have to stop and catch myself. Mainly because of improper neurological feedback, learning to walk would take time because nothing could be done to speed up the healing process on my damaged nerves. The doctors had told me this healing would take up to five years and that there was no guarantee that my nerves would ever fully heal. In fact, normally the chance of their completely healing would be infinitesimal. But mine was not a textbook case. I'd defied the odds on almost everything else, so doctors were reluctant to offer a guess.

I felt that the final major area that needed work was my speech. But, like my damaged nerves, the damage done to my vocal cords and larynx would take time to heal. The doctors and therapists agreed that I should wait at least another year before attempting to work on this area.

Although there were countless other problems, these were my most immediate concerns. If I could concentrate on these areas with the same degree of intensity I'd used to achieve previous goals, I'd be doing just fine.

It was the middle of January when I saw Dr. Rish for my first post-discharge appointment. Four months earlier, I'd seen him while I'd been home for my week-long stay. At that time, I could barely shuffle my feet forward with the aid of a walker, and my hands were stiff, clenched, and fairly useless.

This time it was different. You should have seen his face when I walked into his office, without the walker, and extended my hand to shake his.

"I told you I would walk into your office and shake your hand," I reminded him.

"You sure did," he replied. "But I never would have believed it in a thousand years." Then Dr. Rish proceeded to examine me from head to toe. I'd become his most famous case, and he wanted to know all the details. To say he seemed shocked and surprised would be an understatement. When I got down on the floor and stood up, it was too much for him.

"I just can't believe it," he said, shaking his head.

"When can I really start working on my shoulder and arm strength?" I inquired. I didn't want to push myself too hard and create more problems.

"It's still too early," he told me. "We don't want to take a chance on breaking your fusion; your neck is still healing. In March we'll take a complete set of X-rays and see how everything looks then. That will be one year from the date of your accident. If everything looks okay, then I'll give your therapists the go-ahead to start working full throttle on your shoulder girdle."

Before I left, I asked him about my Philadelphia Collar. I was still wearing this to support my neck, but it was uncomfortable, and I really hoped that I could get rid of it. Once again, I was told to be patient and bide my time. Well, he's the doctor, I thought. I don't want to risk creating more problems for myself by being overzealous and making things worse.

By the end of January, I was starting to get around a little better. So one Sunday, I decided to visit the intensive care unit at Norfolk General Hospital and see all my old nurses. Sandy and I arrived and headed upstairs on the elevator. As the doors opened, I reflected on the touch-and-go days just ten months ago. Now, here I was, standing on my own two feet, walking down those same halls where I'd traveled on a stretcher, connected to tubes and monitors.

The nurses were astonished; their reactions were written all over their faces. Even in their wildest imaginations, none of them had ever thought they would see me again, much less standing there on my own.

"I promised you I'd return," I said smiling, "and here I am." Because many of the nurses who'd cared for me were on a different shift, I said I'd return in a few weeks and try to see them then. All in all, it was a wonderful homecoming.

February started out miserably. The severely cold, damp, and windy weather kept me confined to the house most of the time. All I needed was to slip on a patch of ice and break something else. My bankruptcy proceedings were progressing much more slowly than I had hoped. My financial problems, as well as the outside environment, were creating a lot of stress.

I called Mel Friedman and pleaded with him to get things going faster. He suggested contacting another attorney who specialized in bankruptcies, and I gave him my okay. Do anything you can to finalize the situation, I told him. Added to my physical stress, this problem was becoming just too much to handle. I wanted it finished, soon.

To help counter the effects of the stress, I was building up my vitamin and nutrition program. I was taking quite a number of vitamins at this point, a practice most doctors think is simply a waste of time. They'll never sell that idea to me. I was feeling better, physically and mentally, and I was sure that this was due to a corrective program of diet and nutritional supplements.

But my spirits didn't stay down for long. One evening, while watching television, I got a phone call from my aunt, Goldie Mogul.

"I was talking with Butch Pierce today, and he asked me if I thought you would be willing to give the invocation at the Tidewater Sales Congress," she said.

"That's quite an honor," I replied. "I'd be more than happy to do it." She gave me his home number and asked if I would give Butch a call. Thurman B. (Butch) Pierce was in charge of this year's congress, an annual event sponsored by the Norfolk

Life Underwriters. This all-day affair always featured noted speakers from all over the country. I was really excited.

That night I called Butch and accepted his invitation. On Friday, February 19, at the Omni Hotel in downtown Norfolk, I would address my fellow underwriters. Nothing short of death or another tragedy could have prevented me from being there.

When the big day arrived, Sandy drove me to the hotel and dropped me off. My old friend, Doug Martin, who was there as an exhibitor, was to take me home later.

The pain that day was very bad, and it was all I could do to make it there. Originally, I'd planned on staying for the entire meeting, but that morning I knew that as soon as I finished giving the invocation, I would ask Doug to take me home.

How disappointing! I had really wanted to stay and hear Frank E. Sullivan speak. Frank is a legend in the insurance business. He's won every award possible. I'd never met Frank, but he"d been a hero of mine ever since my early days in insurance sales. I'd just wanted to shake his hand.

As Butch introduced me, the room settled into a solemn stillness. Two of my fellow underwriters helped me onto the stage, and I began the prayer.

Dear Heavenly Father, thank You for bringing us together today. Let it be a day of learning, new wisdom, and better understanding of ourselves and our fellow man. In the coming year, we ask not for opportunity equal to our ability, but rather that you help each of us to acquire ability equal to the opportunity that will come our way. Oh Heavenly Father, look over our speakers, who so unselfishly have given of their time and talent. Let their words ring out to each of us and inspire us to reach a little higher. And, dear God, for those out there who are thinking of leaving this great business, please direct them my way so that I can open my heart and tell them about what this business, and so many of the people in it, have meant to me over the past eleven months. I do not know how I would have hung on without the prayers and thoughts of my fellow underwriters and without the knowledge that, through the wonder of life insurance, my family would be well cared for if anything happened to me. Dear Heavenly Father, I feel we have come to know each other well the last eleven months. And if I can have just one prayer answered, it is that You be as good to everyone here today during the coming year as You have been to me over the past year. Amen.

Suddenly everyone rose up and applauded—an unusual occurrence after an invocation! For several minutes, 600 people clapped and cried. Then I walked over to shake hands with Frank Sullivan. We had a wonderful little conversation while things settled down, and we began an endearing friendship.

Frank told me that my invocation was the most inspiring introduction to a meeting he'd ever heard. At future events, several people mentioned that never, in all of the hundreds of meetings they'd attended, had they seen anyone get a standing ovation for an invocation. I simply told them that it was just God speaking to everyone through me.

March was just around the corner; soon it would be a full year since my accident. Progress in therapy was slow but steady. Week in and week out, it was the same routine—occupational therapy, physical therapy, acupuncture treatments, and working out at home in my gym. I had the wrist machine Page Scott had made for me, the sander built by Bill Hermann, and a complete home gym and exercise machine. I also had barbells, dumbbells, and ankle and wrist weights. If I ever finished my rehabilitation program, I'd have the opportunity to get into fine physical shape!

Dr. Rish's office called to set up an appointment for me to have my neck X-rayed in early March. We decided that I would have them done on an outpatient basis at nearby Bayside Hospital before I came in for my examination. He'd call the hospital to arrange for the necessary X-rays, I'd have them taken, and then carry them with me to his office.

On March 4, I walked into Dr. Rish's waiting room, handed the X-rays to his nurse, and sat down to wait for the doctor to see me. After a routine examination, Dr. Rish asked that I have a seat in his office. When he came in with the X-rays, I took a deep breath and hoped for the best. He sat down behind his desk and looked straight at me.

"Your films look good," he said. "I think you can go full ahead with your exercise program. I'll call Diane Petry and give her the okay."

"Will I be able to raise my arms over my head again?" I asked. Well, Dr. Rish wouldn't commit himself on that one. He said I'd just have to wait and see. That answer wasn't surprising, but I was surprised at myself for asking the question. I was leaving myself open to be SNIOP'ed. As if that weren't bad enough, I asked *another* question.

"Will I ever be able to go hunting again?" I inquired. This time he was emphatic.

"You will never be able to shoot a gun again," he insisted. "The recoil would be too much for your neck to stand."

I closed my mind, refusing to hear what he was saying. I'd hunted all my life, and I knew that it was the shoulder, not the neck, that took most of the recoil. Besides, I'd heard about a man named Edwards, who'd invented the Edward's Recoil Reducer. By taking away part of the gun stock and by installing two cylinders that acted as shock absorbers, the recoil was reduced to practically nothing.

I decided then and there to write him as soon as I got home. Of course, I would have to strengthen my arms and shoulder enough to *mount* a gun—right now I couldn't raise them, let alone support eight or nine pounds. So this was my next goal. I would give it all the energy and concentration I could muster, and the way I felt after Dr. Rish's comments, that was plenty.

March 10, the first anniversary of my accident, was a difficult day. My mind kept drifting back to the crash—the wires, the impact of the crash, the ambulance ride, the arrival at the hospital, the look of horror on everyone's face. It was all crystal clear. That evening I spoke with my mother, sister, and in-laws.

"Let's hope this will be a better year for all of us," said Mother Fink just before she hung up.

"I sure hope so," I replied. The accident had taken a heavy toll on Sandy's parents. For their sakes, I hoped that there would be no more tragedies in the family. Fate did not cooperate.

While Sandy and I were watching television on Saturday night, March 13, the phone rang. Sandy answered it, and I could tell by her tone of voice, as well as by the "Oh, God" and "How?" comments on her side of the conversation, that something was wrong.

"What is it? What's the matter?" I asked her.

"It's my sister," Sandy murmured. "Debbie is dying." Then she ran downstairs to use the kitchen phone so that I could get on the line, too. My whole body felt numb as I took the receiver from her.

"What's happening?" I asked. Mother and Dad were crying so much that I could barely understand them.

"It's Debbie," they sobbed. "Our Debbie is dying. The doctors say she won't make it through the night." After probing some more, I found out that Debbie had contracted some type of blood disease that the doctors couldn't identify. It had taken over her entire system, and she had lapsed into a coma.

Debbie had gone for a checkup the week before. The doctor was not in, so a nurse had performed the exam. She took a Pap smear and commented that she saw a germ that she'd never seen before. But no further tests were done, and Debbie was sent home with some medication. Debbie hadn't mentioned this incident to Mom and Dad, and she had made only a casual comment about it to a girl friend. Now she was deathly ill and in a hospital.

As soon as Sandy's folks hung up, I called the airlines to see when the next day's flights were scheduled; it was too late that night to catch a flight. We decided that Sandy would go home to be with her parents, and I would stay with my sister or an aunt. I was in no condition to make such a trip. But if Debbie died and there was a funeral, I was going anyway.

I lined up a flight for the next day and then called Mom and Dad back. We agreed to stay in touch throughout the night. If there were any changes in Debbie's condition, they would call us.

All night long, I was in a state of shock. Debbie was only 27 years old. And she was a new mother, too. On November 10, just three days before my discharge and a day after my birthday, she'd delivered a healthy baby boy. Now she might never get to see him grow up. It didn't seem possible. Sandy and her parents weren't fully recovered from the shock of my accident—and now this. It just wasn't fair.

About 9:00 the next morning, Mom and Dad called, and we told them about the day's plan. My clothes were packed, and Aunt Lena had agreed to let me stay with her until Sandy returned. My sister, Pat, was coming to pick us up, take Sandy to the airport, and drive me to my aunt's house. But Dad told Sandy not to come just yet. There had been a slight improvement in Debbie's condition overnight. He'd call us back if she changed one way or the other.

Debbie was still on the critical list, though, so the doctors had warned us not to get our hopes up too high. But after what I'd made it through, all of us realized that anything was possible. In a way, this was a cruel trick on us. Mom and Dad were looking for another miracle, another one-in-a-million shot. So Sandy delayed her trip for the time being, and we kept in touch almost daily with her parents for the next few weeks. There were moments when it looked as if things might be turning in Debbie's favor, but then she would regress further.

By the middle of April, she was on total life-support systems, and numerous tests showed no brain function whatever. The doctors pronounced her legally dead. Still Mom and Dad held on. They told themselves over and over again that where there was life, there was hope.

I said nothing to convince them that it was all over, but I knew in my heart that Debbie was with us in body only. Her soul and spirit were now with God.

About this same time, Susan Morales decided that she'd done all she could for me. She placed me on a maintenance program and told me to call her if I needed anything. My right hand was now at a functional level. My left was still very spastic. But Susan felt that she'd done everything possible, so it was up to Mother Nature and the Lord from this point on. She'd done a fine job. At our last appointment, I thanked her for her help and assured her that I would continue my exercises and keep in touch.

The burning and pain in my legs, however, were showing no signs of improvement. Driving back and forth to Portsmouth three times a week was taking its toll on Sandy and me. Was it worth it? When I expressed my concerns to Dr. Su, he told me that he knew of another doctor who practiced acupuncture, Dr. Gerald Acierto. His office was located in Norfolk, only a 15-minute drive from my house. So I asked Dr. Su to call him and arrange for an appointment. Within a week, I was transferred over to Dr. Acierto's care. His methods were the same as Dr. Su's, but he tried different nerve points. Still, I felt little, if any, relief. For the time being, though, I had no other alternatives; until I could try another method of treatment, I would stick with this one and hope that it would help.

Thank goodness for the month of May and the warmer weather. Now I could get out of the house more to get some fresh air. My busy schedule of therapy sessions continued, but somehow the mild, sweet-smelling air, blooming flowers, and sunny days made it all easier to bear.

One day I stopped by Landon Browning's office for a visit. He told me that a new doctor had just moved into his office complex. After Landon had described my case to him the doctor said how interested he was in meeting with me. His name was Dr. Jack Kenley, and he was a chiropractor. I was less than enthusiastic. I guess I had the usual misconceptions about these specialists—that they aren't *real* doctors, that they're no better than a masseur, that people who go to see them are being taken.

Well, several weeks passed before I finally decided to talk with him, more out of courtesy to Landon than anything else. By the time I left Dr. Kenley's office, I had a totally different perspective. He seemed knowledgeable, intelligent, and had a good grasp of my condition. And I loved his attitude. I'd seen so many doctors by now that I could tell after asking just a few questions whether or not they understood my condition or were just shooting from the hip. Dr. Kenley spoke my language. He didn't promise me the moon, but his positive attitude and approach made quite an impression on me.

I agreed to let him work on my case to see what would happen. Jack wanted to see me every day for two weeks, then we would sit down and discuss further treatment based on the results I'd achieved up to that point.

From those two weeks, things were unbelievably hectic. Monday, Wednesday, and Friday, I had physical therapy from 9:00 until 10:30, saw Dr. Kenley from 11:00 until 1:00, ate lunch, saw Dr. Acierto at 2:30, and finally got home about 5:00. On Tuesday and Thursday, it wasn't as bad because I'd see Dr. Kenley from 10:00 until noon and still have the afternoon free to work out at home. At least we didn't have to drive to Portsmouth anymore.

Halfway through the month of May, Jack and I had our discussion. He felt that he could help me, but it would be a long slow process. Over the previous two weeks, I hadn't gotten any relief from the pain, yet my confidence in Jack and my need to continue trying everything possible led me to keep up the treatments.

We settled on Monday, Wednesday, and Friday as my

regular appointment days. This was a heavy burden on Sandy, but it left her free on Tuesdays and Thursdays. Once we'd adjusted to our new schedule, Sandy decided to volunteer as a nurse's aide at Bayside Hospital in Virginia Beach. Before our marriage, she'd worked as a kindergarden teacher and an assistant nurse. Now Sandy wanted to have the opportunity to put to use all the information she had gathered from caring for me, and she needed to get out and be with other people, too. It also helped to keep her mind off her sister, Debbie.

Through May and June, Debbie seemed to be getting worse with each passing day. We were usually in touch with Sandy's parents twice a week or more. The news was always grim. Debbie was being kept alive by machines, and soon a decision would have to be made about disconnecting her from the machines. Letting her go was going to be very hard. Luckily, Debbie's husband, Dale, seemed to be coping with the situation much better than Mom and Dad.

I think Dad realized that there was now no hope for Debbie. But Mom refused to give up. She'd believed that I'd pull through when everyone else thought that it was all over for me. She'd witnessed a miracle, and she was praying for another.

When it was time for Debbie to be disconnected from her life-support systems, Mom and Dad asked us to come down and see her. No one knew how quickly she'd deteriorate once she was cut loose from all those machines. This visit was really important to Sandy's parents, so we decided that I'd go along.

We arrived in Durham, North Carolina, on Friday afternoon. It was the first time Sandy and I'd seen her parents since Debbie had gotten sick. Embracing each other tightly, we all cried. That night, we realized how hard Debbie's illness was hitting Mom and Dad. All night long, they walked the floor and cried. I'd never seen them in such a state. Usually they were happy, smiling, and outgoing, but now it was as if all the joy in their lives was being eaten away, devoured by an all-consuming sorrow.

On Saturday we drove to Winston Salem to take one last look at Debbie. Seeing her lying there, a corpse kept alive by machines, was just heartbreaking. It is an image I cannot forget.

Sandy and I returned home to await the outcome. There was no way to avoid the realization that our next trip to Durham would be for Debbie's funeral.

By the middle of the summer, my bankruptcy proceedings still hadn't been finalized. I felt as if my life was in constant turmoil. My financial problems, the constant pain, my continual struggle to reconstruct my life and overcome my disability, and, of course, Debbie's impending death, were pushing me to the breaking point.

My progress in physical therapy had slowed and then reached a plateau. Lately, I'd seen very little improvement in my upper body strength. Oh, I could get my right arm up to chin level well enough; but my left arm still wouldn't go any higher than 20°. Diane had done a commendable job in getting me back to a more functional level. However, neither she nor any other therapists nor doctors I contacted, could say why my arms did not respond better. Perhaps it was due to muscle atrophy and counterspasticity or to lost-nerve conduction. I didn't want hypotheses, I wanted action. I decided to stop seeing Diane for treatments. While continuing to work out in my own gym, I would look for another solution.

Dr. Kenley suggested an EMG (electromyograph) to determine if proper nerve impulses were being transmitted to my shoulders and deltoids. This was something Diane had suggested several times, but when I had asked Dr. Rish about it, he just shrugged it off as unnecessary.

Then, in early August, I received an appointment reminder in the mail for an EMG. It was to be performed at Tidewater Rehabilitation Institute by Dr. Charles R. Peterson, and it had been ordered by Dr. Rish. What a surprise!

The test was simple. Needles were placed in various parts of my shoulder and arm to measure whether sufficient nerve impulses were being transmitted to my muscles. All the test results were in the normal range. Armed with this information, Dr. Kenley and I sat down to discuss our next move. He spent several hours doing a complete muscle evaluation on my entire body.

Jack determined that my shoulder girdle and deltoids were a grade one. This meant that there was some contraction in my muscles but not enough to do any active resistance exercises or to use weights. So we would take a different approach. By using high-voltage currents fed directly into my muscles, we could force them to contract, thus giving them the exercise they needed to increase my strength. Once their contracting power was improved, we could begin using weights.

One thing Dr. Kenley really helped me with was my Philadelphia Collar. The old one was made of styrofoam, covered with cloth, and because it had been cut to fit instead of being made to a certain size, it never fit quite right. Jack gave me a new one, similar in design, but made of cloth and straps that could be adjsted to the proper tension. It was great to eliminate that added extra pain in the neck; oh, my neck still bothered me, but at least the support didn't!

As summer came to a close, I decided to stop seeing Dr. Acierto. He'd done his best, but the burning just would not subside. Everyone told me that I would have to learn to live with it. However, Dr. Kenley was more optimistic. He constantly telephoned people all over the country trying to find an answer to my problem. So far, I hadn't felt any improvement from his treatments, either, but because of his positive attitude, I stuck with him.

By now I was adjusting rather well to my situation. Recognizing that I would have to work on my rehabilitation for a long time to come, I refused to let myself get discouraged when I couldn't walk as far or reach as high or handle a task as well as I wanted to. Still, something was missing in my life—fun. It had been so long since I'd gone fishing and hunting. If there was any way at all that I could handle a fishing reel or mount a gun, I was going to do it. Mere existence wasn't enough; I was going to start enjoying life again.

chapter **11**

OUTDOORS AGAIN

"There is a passion for hunting something
deeply implanted in the human breast."

CHARLES DICKENS

Every day during the eight months that I had been hospitalized, I visualized myself hunting and fishing again. Being an outdoorsman had been a vital part of my life since I'd been knee high to a grasshopper. Unlike a hobby that a person tries and discards for the next passing fancy, hunting and fishing gets into the blood. It's for keeps.

Now that I was home, it was even harder to accept my limitations—mostly a lack of upper body strength that hampered my ability to handle a fishing reel or a gun. I was ready to see what I could do. My blood raced every time I read something in the paper about spot fishing or when I talked with Dr. Oden. Because my hands had improved, I was sure that I could hold a rod and reel, but I didn't know whether I'd have the strength and control to wind in a spot. It was time to find out.

I arranged a fishing trip with Dr. Oden on his new boat in August. When I arrived at the boat via a taxi he'd sent over from one of his cab companies, I discovered that another old friend, Albert Russell, was going with us.

Before long the three of us were headed out to sea. What a grand feeling it was. I finally felt as if I was a part of it all once again—a part of living, not just a part of life. That day I didn't really care whether or not I caught any fish. But catch fish I did. By the end of the outing, I'd caught 54 spot by myself. My hands were sore and bruised from the unaccustomed use, so bruised that I could no longer open and close them, but it was well worth it. I must have truly been possessed that day. Leonard and Albert caught about 60 spot—together.

That evening we stopped by Leonard's house, and his wife, Ginny, fried some fresh spot for us. While eating some of our catch, my companions told her how well I'd done. Ginny was quite happy for me.

"You never could beat him," she chuckled to Leonard.

"Nope," I agreed. "He couldn't beat me before, and he can't beat me now." At this, we all had a good laugh.

Leonard, Albert, and I went spot fishing two more times during the early days of September. It was thrilling to have some joy returning to my life. But there was to be more sorrow as well.

On Monday, September 13, Debbie passed away. Sandy and I made the trip back to Durham, a trip that we had known was coming. Mom and Dad were beside themselves, completely shattered by the tragedy that had struck so soon after the shock of my accident. For the first time in my life, I did not know what to say. Words would have been of little consolation anyway—only time would heal their wounds of grief.

The funeral was on Wednesday in Winston Salem, where Debbie had been hospitalized. A letter written by Debbie's husband, Dale, added a beautifully touching moment to the rabbi's eulogy. It was a heartbreaking situation—a young woman, not yet in the prime of life, taken from an infant son, a loving husband, and parents, who were already under the strain of a recent disaster.

We stayed with Mom and Dad until Saturday. Then Sandy and I headed for home once more. Immersing ourselves in our daily routines would help to ease the pain of our loss, and although Sandy's folks wanted us to stay longer, they had friends and relatives to comfort them and had their own lives to piece together again.

Little things that most of us take for granted were still giving me difficulty. Take swallowing. How many of us think about the physical act of eating? But for me, I *had* to think about it or I'd choke to death. Swallowing wasn't an automatic reflex for me because of the damage done to my throat. Oh, most of the time, it didn't take an enormous amount of conscious thought to swallow, but I couldn't talk and eat at the same time. And this condition will never change.

And I couldn't raise my arms over my head yet. My right arm was getting much better, but my left was not very useful. I worked like a driven man on improving this. If I wanted to go hunting, I would not only need to lift up my arms but also be able to hold up nine pounds worth of gun. Dr. Rish had been concerned about the recoil of a gun and thought I would never be able to shoot again. I knew that wasn't so, but a special gun would help. With a regular stock, I couldn't look down the barrel to aim because I couldn't bend my neck properly—

when I put my head down to the barrel, it would fall off to the right instead of forward, so the gun would end up pointing way out to the left side of my face. The lighter the gun, the easier it would be on me, so I would have to go to a smaller bore gun. This would reduce the recoil, but it would also reduce the power and effective distance of the gun.

I was thinking about all these special requirements when I read an article in *Field and Stream* about the Reinhart Fajen Gunstock Corporation in Warsaw, Missouri. This company has a large factory that employs 60 people whose specialty is gun stocks. I wrote to them in November and explained my problem and the type of stock I needed. Six months later, I flew out there to see what they could do.

During the two days I was there, two of the best men at the plant were assigned to work with me. They made a model stock out of a liquid wood, which can be built up or sanded down. Once they got something that fit me well, I went back home, leaving my gun with them.

I'd done a lot of research before I bought this particular gun. All my life, I'd shot a 12-gauge. But the weight and recoil would be more than I could take right now, so I searched for the lightest automatic shotgun I could find. This turned out to be a Banelli 20-gauge by Heckler and Koch, which has half the recoil of a 12-gauge and weighs only 5 pounds 10 ounces.

When the gun arrived in July 1983, I was pleased to find that it was a perfect fit. They had made the stock out of white maple, the lightest hardwood available, and had hollowed it out to keep its weight to a minimum. The stock also had a thick recoil pad on the end of it, with an adjustable plate that moved up and down so it fit my shoulder.

As soon as I had looked it over, I sent the gun to Stan Baker in Seattle, Washington. Stan is reputed to be the best gunsmith in the world, so I entrusted him with the final custom work. He bored some holes in the end of the barrel to help further reduce the recoil, he opened up the chamber, and he made some special tubes. By the time I got my gun back in September, I'd built up enough strength to hold it up and shoot it completely on my own.

Now I had to practice—I hadn't shot a gun in almost two years. Before the accident, I'd been a first-class competitive trap and skeet shooter, but now, with muscles to retrain and eye-hand coordination to redevelop, I thought that some professional help was necessary. I enrolled in the Orvis Shooting School, located in Manchester, Vermont. I didn't know what to expect, but it seemed as if it was worth a try. After all, this was a school that had been patterned after the world-famous Holland and Holland School of England. If anybody could help me, Orvis could.

So, during the second week of September, off I went. I was very pleased with the individualized attention. There were 15 people taking lessons and five instructors, so there were only three students to a class. They had several courses set up to resemble hunting situations, and each class alternated on these courses. For instance, one time we walked through the woods, and skeets came out from the left and right, then in front of us, and behind us.

On the second day of class, my classmates were a neurologist from Casper, Wyoming, and a veterinarian from New York. Malvin Cole, the neurologist, couldn't believe that anyone with my injury was even walking around, much less shooting a shotgun. His amazement increased once we finished that day's course. The veterinarian, Alfred Grossman, went first, and he got three out of the ten targets. Then Malvin went, and he got two out of ten. When it was my turn, I got all ten.

"That's not too bad for a cripple, is it?" I said with a jovial snicker.

"That's not bad for *anybody*," said Malvin. He told me that he was going back home and changing his approach. Never again would he tell patients with spinal cord injuries that they could never do anything. A few weeks later, after we'd all returned home, I received a note from Malvin and a copy of the following letter:

September 28, 1983

Mr. Richard G. High
Editor, Casper Star-Tribune
170 Star Lane
Casper, Wyoming 82601

Dear Sir:
Secretary Watt never, of course, has to worry about becoming a woman, black or Jewish, but as far as that other member of

his commission goes, he, like the rest of us, is not immune.
As a neurologist, the word "cripple" has special importance.
A recent past director of the Veterans Administration, who
was himself a triple amputee, stated that he was not disabled,
only inconvenienced. Recently, I saw a gentlemen with a very
severe spinal cord injury affecting all four limbs shoot a
shotgun more accurately than most of us are able to. To be
"crippled" is a state of mind. It is not having a physical
inconvenience. I have many patients with physical
inconveniences and for whom the term cripple has no
bearing. I repeat, the word has to do with the state of mind
and that state of mind may be a better description of the
Secretary than of members of the commission.

Yours truly,

Malvin Cole, M.D.

The Vererans Administration administrator was Max Cleland
and, of course, the gentleman with the shotgun was me. Malvin's letter ran in the Casper *Star-Tribune* on October 2, 1983.
Once again I felt that perhaps I was helping someone besides
myself with my positive thinking and determination.

On November 10, Dr. Oden and I went to Maryland to
hunt geese. We had a fantastic time, and we each got three
geese, the allowable limit. To come from a condition where I
could only lie flat on my back, to this—actually shooting a gun
again—was the fulfillment of a dream I'd had since I realized
that I wasn't dead. There had been many other goals that needed
to be met before I could even attempt this one, but the time
had come, and I'd made it.

My walking had improved to the point where I could go
for a distance of three or four miles on my own—no wheelchair,
walker, or cane. But my balance was still impaired, and I had
a particularly hard time going up and down stairs. During the
week before Thanksgiving, I found out just how much of a
problem this was. As I was going down the steps of an office
building, I lost my balance. When I got to the bottom of the
steps, still on my feet but out of control, I kept on going. The
sidewalk was on a hill, and I reeled forward. When I finally
stopped, I'd fallen against a car so hard that I put a dent in the

side of it. My head was bleeding, my knees and elbows and arms were skinned, one eye was black, and my face was scratched. They had to come and get me in an ambulance.

I was sure that I'd really hurt myself this time, but nothing was broken, and I was sent home. The doctor told me I was the toughest man he'd ever seen; he didn't think anything was going to kill me. Well, I'm not so sure about *that*, and I'm more careful on steps now. I had a headache for about a week. As you know by now, though, I'm used to pain, so I went hunting that weekend anyway.

Today, the beginning of 1984, I am still trying to reach that all-important goal of full recovery. My therapy schedule remains intense and time-consuming. On Monday, Wednesday, and Friday, I wake up at 6:00 A.M. and crawl on the floor for about thirty minutes, using a cross/crawl board, which is a special exercise unit with four pegs, one for each hand and knee, to place yourself on so that when you crawl, you don't actually go anywhere. The purpose of this is to get the pattern of left arm/right leg, right arm/left leg back into the brain. Infants do this naturally, as a prerequisite to walking. Now I needed to reteach my brain so that I could walk with less difficulty. I have been doing this since August 1983.

At 9:00, I go to physical therapy and work until about 10:30. Then I see Dr. Kenley for more therapy and pain-control treatment. This treatment lasts until about 12:00 or 12:30. After lunch, I crawl again and work out in my gym.

On Tuesday, Thursday, and Saturday, I crawl for about 30 minutes three times a day (morning, noon, and before bed) and do some weight lifting to develop upper body strength. On Sundays, except for the crawling exercise three times a day, I rest. I must admit that sometimes hunting and fishing cancel my Saturday and Sunday schedule.

One of my main goals right now is to improve my balance so that my walking will improve. My left side is still impaired for several reasons. First, the leg muscles on my left side are much weaker than those on my right side. So I'm working in therapy to strengthen these muscles. This, however, will not correct the spasticity I suffer along my entire left side. I don't shake all the time, but my muscles contract, making them useless. The toes on my left side tighten up so that I can't set my foot down flat and, therefore, don't get the proper feedback I need to keep my balance. Lately, I have been wearing a device called a respond neuromuscular stimulator. At first I used this to exercise my muscles, but one day I discovered that if I put the self-adhesive pads attached to the two electrodes on certain places on top of my foot, it would straighten my toes. I still don't get the sensory input I need, but at least my foot is easier to walk on. Other muscles on my left side don't know when to contract or expand normally because of improper impulses going from the muscle to my brain. Again, this throws off my balance. In therapy, I am trying to exercise these muscles in the hope of alleviating some of this problem. Finally, my co-ordination is off, so I use the crawl board to help me relearn the necessary right/left pattern for keeping my balance when I'm upright.

My next priority is working on upper body strength. I can now raise my right arm over my head with about three pounds of weight. But even though I can get my left arm over my head only once or twice in the morning, it won't go above chin level. My immediate goal is to raise five pounds over my head with each arm. Naturally, when I accomplish this, I'll go on to in-crease the amount of weight. I can shoulder and shoot my gun with my present capabilities, but I would like to handle a more powerful gun someday.

My efforts in hand therapy have really been rewarded. I finally have full dexterity in my left as well as my right hand. But the speed in my left needs further improvement—when I try to open and close it rapidly, it sometimes cramps. I believe that this condition will get better with use.

And, of course, there is the burning sensation. My chi-ropractic treatments haven't given me much relief, so I continue to hope for a new type of therapy that will eliminate this con-stant pain. Some days, it drives me batty. But I am making progress in other areas and try not to focus on this problem.

One more area that I would like to work on, but haven't yet, is my speech. I've tried to improve it on my own, and most people have no difficulty understanding me. Speech therapy, though, would probably help a great deal. I used to be an accomplished speaker, giving talks all over the country. I used to be a very good guitarist and singer. Talking to other people about my accident and what I've learned from my experiences is really important to me, so I will practice on my own until

I've overcome some of the more pressing physical problems, and then begin an intensive program toward regaining a normal speaking voice. I may never be able to sing as I used to, but I plan on giving it a try, too.

I suppose many people would have given up all this frantic activity by now. Many people believe what others tell them— that they can reach only a certain level of competence or success or wealth, and then that's it, there's no use in trying to do more. I'm not one of those people.

Today I can do most of the things normal people can do. I just got my driver's license, and I hope to buy a car. I can walk well enough to get around and can function at home without needing someone to be there all the time. I can eat, write, type, dial a phone, dress, and do a hundred other things that all of us take for granted once we learned how to do them during our childhood.

My bankruptcy proceedings are still not finalized. I filed a Chapter 11 bankruptcy, which means that I will pay back every penny I owe. I believe this is the moral thing to do. Every month I receive $3,000 from premiums on insurance policies I'd sold in the past, and it goes right to the bank. In addition, I am going to be selling some property, so I hope to pay off my remaining debt of $80,000 over the next year. I lost many material possessions, including my boat, *Miss Sash*, during this ordeal. Some day I hope to buy another boat so that I can fish as often as I used to.

My disability insurance pays me $3,000 a month, which I use for daily living expenses. Luckily, my excellent medical coverage with Integon and Union Mutual has covered all of my medical bills. If I had had to pay these expenses, or even part of them—they totaled close to $250,000—I would have been completely ruined financially. I hope to regain my former standard of living if I succeed in winning my case against the company that made the plane I was flying, and against the engine manufacturer—a $10 million lawsuit.

My wife and I are having difficulties. Whatever the outcome, I will always appreciate the many months she stood by me. Her love and tenderness kept me going when my handicaps seemed to be bringing my life down around me like a crumbling building.

And I still have dreams. I wasn't kidding when I told Dr.

Bolander, just before I'd left The Towers for Woodrow Wilson, that I would go out and shoot an elephant. Next year I want to go on a safari in Africa. I am already looking into having a special gun made for the trip. Is this impossible? Probably not. Am I convinced that I can do it? Yes. It is not the difficulty of a task that stops most people—it is how difficult they *perceive* it to be. There are some things that I can't do today, maybe I won't even be able to do them in two or three years, but I surely won't be able to do them *ever* if that's what I believe.

Today I am doing well. Tomorrow I hope to do better. This is not a blind, undirected hope, nor a castles-in-the-sky fantasy. It is a focused, concentrated, concrete plan backed up by hard work and a fierce determination to succeed. I want to show others how they can get this kind of hope and keep it. Through personal encounters, books, magazine articles, speaking engagements, and other media that will allow me to touch other people's lives, I want to demonstrate the power of positive thinking and self-belief. Human beings have the wonderful capacity to learn from others. They don't have to go through something themselves to learn from an experience. My life was changed by tragedy. Maybe yours can be changed by reading about it. I hope so.

EPILOGUE

"The meaning of life is to find value in what we do."

GERHARD GSCHWANDTNER

Soon it will be three years since my accident: three years since I began this struggle to live a life worth living. And my struggle will not end, not until I meet the Lord again and He tells me that I have finished the tasks He sent me back to complete on that fateful day in March.

I don't want to preach to you. I'm not a preacher. But I *am* a salesman, and I want to sell you on yourself. To me, success means using all of the abilities and talents given to you by Almighty God to their fullest. To you, God may not even exist, but your abilities and talents do. And you can't possibly use them to the fullest if you don't believe in yourself.

In order to get everything in life you want, you must give life everything you've got. Certainly it was a miracle that I survived the crash, survived the neck surgery, survived the bouts of pneumonia, even survived the close calls with my electric wheelchair (remember the crash with Delores, and the stairwell I almost fell down?). These events happened, and I survived them, but they were out of my control. Other miracles, however, simply wouldn't have happened without an enormous amount of effort on my part. I refused to accept living life as a vegetable. So I did breathing exercises, practiced speaking, tried to eat, and worked hard on improving my mobility until I got results. I could have given up and avoided the extra pain of therapy, but I didn't. I could have let myself be SNIOP'ed (susceptible to the negative influence of other people) into believing that I would never function like a normal human being ever again. I didn't.

You don't have to be SNIOP'ed either. I don't have more positive-thinking cells or better immunity to despair than you do. I just use more of the capacity each one of us has, deep inside, to overcome obstacles. I believe, as Dr. Norman Vincent Peale does, that "every problem contains the seed to its solution." It takes energy, it takes determination, and it takes concentration.

If you are constantly overwhelmed with "oughts" and "shoulds," sit back and ask yourself why. The answer is probably this: too many goals or goals that are too vague, too broad, too complex. So pick one goal. Then define it, narrow it, and break it down into manageable steps. I couldn't eat or speak before I could breathe. I couldn't walk until I could sit up in a wheelchair, stand up by myself, and take those first steps with the aid of a walker. Success takes time and effort.

Maybe you have a specific goal, but subconsciously you're talking yourself out of it, telling yourself that you just can't see yourself accomplishing it. Try using your imagination. Visualize yourself succeeding, reaching your goal. Next, write out a description of what it will be like to achieve your goal, or draw a picture, if you have the use of your hands. Then replay that picture or rethink that description over and over again. Finally, act as if you have already succeeded. I guess my friends and family felt sorry for me when they watched me try to brush my teeth. I couldn't squeeze the toothpaste out of the tube, and I did a messy job of brushing. But I saw myself doing it, and I played this picture over and over again in my mind. I believed I could already do it, and eventually I did.

Expectations are a must. But they have to be *your* expectations. In my case, most of the expectations of others were rather negative. Shortly after the accident, one doctor told a friend of mine that it would have been better for all concerned if I had just been left to die in the tangled wreckage. If I had accepted the expectations of my doctors, I probably wouldn't be here today. Maybe the expectations of your boss or your spouse or someone else are limiting you. On the other hand, others may have grand expectations for you that you feel you can never achieve. This may make you feel as if you are constantly failing. That's why you need to set your own expectations—positive, constructive ones that you know in your heart you can accomplish.

Just because you have self-expectations doesn't mean that you don't need other people, though. We are all interdependent. The power of positive relationships with loved ones, friends, and business associates can be lifesaving. Sharing and caring can make the struggle of life meaningful and can ease the loneliness and self-doubt we all experience at one time or another. My wife, family, friends, and fellow underwriters pulled me through some of the toughest times of my life. I'm not sure I could have made it without them.

Finally, I would like to quote my friend, Gerhard Gschwandtner, who says that "we can't control life, we can only influence it." When my engine failed, my fate was out of my hands. But when I regained consciousness, I realized that I had a choice. I could either sit back and wait to die, or I could try my darnedest to live to the fullest. I sold myself on life. Instead of withdrawing from the world and giving up, I blinked and smiled and kept on going. Don't be afraid to try, and don't be afraid to fail, because the lesson I learned from my ordeal is this: It doesn't matter how many times you stumble and fall—but how many times you stumble and get up.

BIBLIOGRAPHY

Favorite Motivational Books:

(Morris Goodman has over 500 titles in his library.)

Ash, Mary K., *Mary Kay.* New York: Harper and Row, 1981.

Bettger, Frank. *How I Raised Myself from Failure to Success in Selling.* Englewood Cliffs, N.J.: Prentice-Hall, Inc., 1952.

Bristol, Claude M. *The Magic of Believing.* New York: Simon & Schuster, 1973.

Carnegie, Dale. *How to Win Friends and Influence People.* New York: Pocket Books, 1973.

Conwell, Russell H. *Acres of Diamonds.* Englewood Cliffs, N.J.: Prentice-Hall, Inc., 1967.

Danforth, William H. *I Dare You.* Chicago: Success Unlimited, Inc., 1975.

Dyer, Dr. Wayne W. *Pulling Your Own Strings.* New York: Cromwell Co., 1978.

———. *Your Erroneous Zones.* New York: Funk and Wagnalls, 1976.

Gifford, Frank and Mangel, Charles. *Gifford on Courage.* New York: Fell Publishers, Inc., 1975.

Gschwandtner, Gerhard. *Superachievers—Portraits of Success from Personal Selling Power.* Englewood Cliffs, N.J.: Prentice-Hall, Inc., 1984.

Hill, Napoleon. *Think and Grow Rich.* Englewood Cliffs, N.J.: Prentice-Hall, Inc., 1972.

———. *You Can Work Your Own Miracles.* Greenwich, Connecticut: Fawcett Publications, Inc., 1971.

Linkletter, Art. *Yes, You Can.* New York: Simon & Schuster, 1979.

———. *Linkletter Down Under.* Englewood Cliffs, N.J.: Prentice-Hall, Inc., 1968.

Maltz, Maxwell. *The Magic Power of Self-Image Psychology.* New York: Simon & Schuster, 1973.

Mandino, Og. *The Greatest Miracle in the World*. New York: Fell Publications, 1975.

Peale, Dr. Norman Vincent. *The Power of Positive Thinking*. New York: Prentice-Hall, Inc., 1952.

―――. *Enthusiasm Makes the Difference*. Englewood Cliffs, N.J.: Prentice-Hall, Inc., 1967.

―――. *Positive Imaging—The Powerful Way to Change Your Life*. Old Tappan, N.J.: F. H. Revell, 1982.

Roberts, Cavett. *Success with People through Human Engineering and Motivation*. Chicago: Success Unlimited, Inc., 1976.

Schuller, Dr. Robert. *Peace of Mind Through Possibility Thinking*. Garden City, N.Y.: Doubleday, 1976.

Shook, Robert L. *Winning Images*. New York: Macmillian Publishers, 1977.

Sullivan, Frank E., CLU. *The Critical Path to Sales Success*. Indianapolis: R & R Newkirk, 1975.

Waitley, Dr. Dennis. *The Seeds of Greatness*. Old Tappan, N.J.: F. H. Revell, 1983.

―――. *The Winner's Edge*. New York: Times Books, 1980.

Wilkins, Skip and Dunn, Joseph. *The Real Race*. Virginia Beach, Virginia: JCP Corporation of Virginia, 1981.

Ziglar, Zig. *See You at the Top*. Gretna, La.: Pelican Publications, 1975.

―――. *Dear Family*. Gretna, La.: Pelican Publications, 1984.

appendix

CODE CARDS AND KEYS

Key for Alphabet Card

Instructions for Use: (1 blink—*yes,* 2 blinks—*no*)

1. Ask if the first letter is in box 1 (wait for response), box 2 (wait for response), box 3 (wait), box 4 (wait).
2. After finding correct box, ask if letter is on first line (wait for response) or second line (wait for response).
3. After finding correct line, read the letters of that line and wait for *blink.* He will blink as soon as you say the correct letter.
4. Proceed to the second letter of first word, etc., and then on to second word, third word, etc.

Hints:

If you watch carefully, you can tell which box he is looking at and can probably eliminate the first step of finding the correct box.

Signals: *No* can also be conveyed by shaking head in "no" gesture.
Smile means word is correct and/or end of word.
Flutter of eyelids means end of word.

Example of How to Use Alphabet Card

You: Is it box 1, box 2, box 3? *Blink.*

You: The first letter is in box 3. *Blink.*

You: Is it line 1? (*No response or a clear "no."*), line 2? *Blink.*

You: P, Q, R . . . *Blink.* (The first letter is R.)

Go on to second letter.

Alphabet Card

1

1. A B C

2. D E F

2

1. G H I

2. J K L

3

1. M N O

2. P Q R

4

1. S T U V

2. W X Y Z

Key for Subject Areas

I.

1. *Health*

Ask if he needs Body Card.

Wants to know how he is doing.

Wants a doctor or nurse.

Wants to know about prognosis.

2. *Time*

What time is it?

What day is it?

What is the date today?

Find out if he wants to talk about time in the *past, present,* or *future* in relation to the subject you identify (health, business, etc.).

3. *Feelings*

Needs for expression of emotions such as *fear, frustration, anger, hurt, rejection, happiness, love, confusion, concern, dislike, distrust, pleasure,* etc.

4. *Persons*

Ask if he needs Persons Card. If not, have him spell name of person.

5. *Sports*

May want to talk about current events/sports.

May want newspaper, radio, TV, etc.

II.

1. *Personal Business Matters*

Possible areas:

a. family or friends

b. assets (home, car, boat, plane)

c. insurance/hospitalization

d. finances

e. attorney or accountant

2. *Office/Insurance Business Matters*

Possible areas:

a. business associate or his office personnel

b. attorney or accountant

c. Integon

d. Union Mutual

e. other insurance company (e.g., Metropolitan)

f. office property or assets

g. finances

3. *Recreational Needs*

a. tape recorder, radio, TV, reading material

b. change of view

Key Subject Areas

I

1. My health
2. Time
3. Feelings
4. Person
5. Current news/ sports

II

1. Personal Business matters
2. Office/Insurance Business matters
3. Recreational need
4. Alphabet card

RELATIONSHIPS AND PHONE NUMBERS FOR PERSONS CARD

FAMILY	FRIENDS OR BUSINESS ASSOCIATES	MEDICAL PERSONNEL
1. Sandy Goodman (wife) 481–5420 Sam & Jeanette Fink (in-laws) 2. Pat Paul (sister) H: 623–1487 W: 461–1008 Dare Goodman (mother) 853–7986 Pete Goodman (uncle) 625–7805 Ted Gardner 481–7318 3. Others	1. Joe Leibowitz (Accountant) 499–9922 Mel Friedman (Attorney) 460–6000 2. Fred Day (919) 799–5357 Doug Martin 3. Page Scott 337–3615 Landon Browning 340–4567 Henry Law 499–7041 4. Others Lori (Secretary) 499–7041 Dr. Vashell Leonard Oden	*Doctors* Dr. Rish 623–3303 Dr. Derring *Nurses* Pam Pat Beth Mary Ann Debbie *Others* Respiratory therapist Physical therapist Speech therapist Male attendant

Persons Card

Family	Friends or Business	Medical Personnel
1. Sandy Sam Jeanette	1. Joe Mel	Doctor Nurse Other
2. Pat Mama Uncle Pete Ted	2. Fred Doug	
3. Other Aunt Uncle Cousin	3. Page Landon Henry	
	4. Other	

Key Questions for Persons Card

Is the person a *family member?* Wait for response.

Is the person a *friend or business associate?* Wait for response.

Is the person *medical personnel?* Wait for response.

If the person is a family member or a friend/business person, ask questions such as:

1. Do you want to see that person?
2. Do you want me to tell that person something/call that person?
3. Do you want to know something about that person? (e.g., How is he/she? Where is he/she?, etc.)

If the person is medical personnel, ask questions such as:

1. Do you need a doctor/nurse?
2. Is there a particular doctor/nurse you need?
3. Are you in a state of medical emergency?
4. Do you want me to tell/ask the doctor/nurse something?
5. Is the doctor/nurse the only one who can help you now?

Key for Body Card

The medical concerns will be for either *pain* or *need*.

Questions relating to *pain* are in *red*.

Questions relating to *need* are in *blue*. (After identifying part, ask if the need is for an *itch*. Then proceed.)

Hold up body card and ask:

"Is your concern above the waist?" (Areas 1–5)

"Is your concern below the waist?" (Areas 6–8)

"Is your concern a general or overall (body) concern?" (Area 9)

If it is above the waist, say numbers 1–5 until you identify part.

If it is below the waist, say numbers 6–8 until you identify part.

Then find part on the body card and ask questions.

PART 1—HEAD

Pain—Eyes, nose, mouth, ears, cheeks, chin, head (as in headache)

Need—Eye needs: glasses, cleansing, itch
Nose needs: tube, clean nostrils, itch
Mouth needs: suction mouth, lips dry, mouth dry, mouth needs cleaning, teeth, need for taste/food
Ear needs: clean ears
Hair needs: comb, clean/wash
Face needs: wash
Head needs: turn or move

PART 2—THROAT/NECK

Pain—Pain connected to tracheotomy
Pain in back of neck at site of injury and/or surgery
Pain in throat (e.g., sore throat)

Need—Rub neck, turn head/neck

Body Card

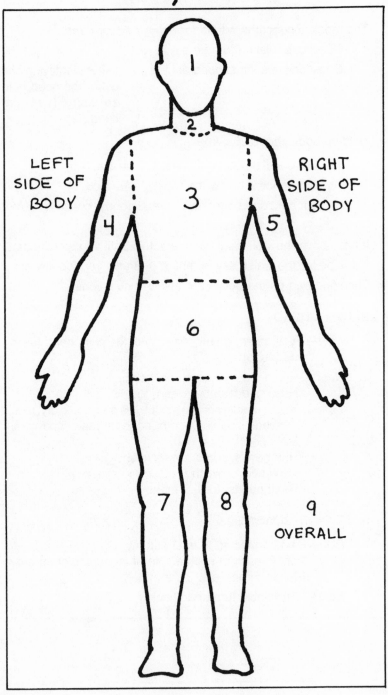

Key for Body Card (continued)

PART 3—CHEST/STOMACH (Ask which. If neither, ask if it is his BACK.)

Chest Pain—Lungs (breathing), ribs, heart

Chest Need—Suction lungs, rub, wash, cough, hot/cold

Stomach Pain—Hunger pain, indigestion, pain in stomach (cause other than hunger or indigestion)

Stomach Need—Food, antacid, rub, wash

Back Pain—Turn body to ease back pain, pain in muscle/ bone

Back Need—Wash, rub, turn *off* of back, turn *onto* back

PART 4 OR PART 5—RIGHT/LEFT SIDE OF BODY (Shoulders, arms [upper, elbow, forearm], hands. Iden- tify part.)

Pain—Move arm or turn shoulder to ease pain/discomfort; cramping muscle, bone pain, sore

Need—Move arm, hand, shoulder
Exercise
Wash, rub, cold/hot (cover, uncover)

PART 6—PELVIS OR INTESTINAL; BUTTOCKS (Identify part.)

Pain—Associated with elimination (urination, bowels)
In rectum/anus; sore buttocks
In penis, urethra; in kidneys or bladder
In testicles

Need—Elimination: urination, bowels; empty urinal/bed pan
Enema
Rectal ointment
Wash, rub

PART 7 OR 8—LEGS (thighs, knees, calves), FEET

Pain—Move leg or foot to ease pain/discomfort; cramping muscle, bone pain, sore

Need—Move leg or foot; need foot support/board
Exercise
Wash, rub, cold/hot (cover, uncover)

Key for Body Card (continued)

PART 9—OVERALL OR GENERAL

Pain—Overall discomfort; aching or sore all over

Need—Cold (cover); hot (uncover); feel feverish
       Need to be turned; move position of bed (head, foot)
       Tired, fatigued, sleepy; low spirits/depressed
       Wash